WICHES

101 Ways to Think
Outside The Lunchbox

Adrian Fiorino
Creator, Insanewiches.com

St. Martin's Griffin
New York

www.stmartins.com

Library of Congress Cataloging-in-Publication Data Available
Upon Request
ISBN: 978-0-312-66884-6

10 9 8 7 6 5 4 3 2 1

Produced by The Stonesong Press

First St. Martin's Griffin Edition August 2011

Designed by Ohioboy Art & Design

For my parents, Joe and Lina Fiorino

Thank Yous

It's really too bad that only my name appears on the front cover of this book, when a whole bunch of people made it possible. So I'll thank everyone I can think of. Sorry if I missed you.

My literary agent, Judy Linden of The Stonesong Press: Thanks for noticing my blog and for making it into a book. Quite frankly, this book wouldn't exist without your patience (man, you're patient!) and all the hard work you've put in.

The rest of the Stonesong team: Thanks, Katherine Latshaw, Alison Fargis, Ellen Scordato, and everyone else who contributed.

St. Martin's Press: Thanks, B.J. Berti, for your thoughtful comments and solutions, for having an open mind, and for having my bizarre book of sandwiches published.

Erik Trinidad: Many thank yous for posting my Wendy's Napoleon on your site FancyFastFood.com back on July 20, 2009, and for linking back to Insanewiches. This got the ball rolling for me! I'm glad you saw the humor in my submission!

Simon Vallee-Reinhart: Thanks for your hard work with the original site design, for being a source of inspiration and for showing me that bumps in the road are only interruptions, not roadblocks.

Tony Pipilas: Thanks for sharing my strange sense of humor and for encouraging me every crazy step of the way. Thanks also for not thinking I was unstable (I knew you wouldn't) when I first told you about Insanewiches and for listening patiently when I bounced ideas off you.

Diego Fiorino: Thanks for having an encyclopedic knowledge of food, and for letting me call you at all hours with random questions about bread or cheese (and for having an answer even if you were half asleep!).

Pat Fiorino: Thanks for showing me a thing or two about offbeat humor. Many of the sandwiches in this book are inspired by the crazy, wacky humor we share.

Joe Fiorino: Thanks for being the voice of reason and for helping me out with technical issues, especially when Insanewiches got hit so hard it crashed. Thanks also for the inspiring talks and for showing me that breaking the rules is OK.

To my Janet: Thanks for being level-headed, for putting things into perspective, and for your support. I'm grateful for your useful input and, most importantly, for your just being there. Luvs for that. And oh, yeah, thanks for not caring that the kitchen looks like it should be featured on TV's *Destroyed in Seconds* when I'm insanewiching!

Mom and Pop: Thanks for teaching me through example that patience and hard work pay off. Thanks also for feeding me such great meals when I visit, and for raising me in a household where food means more than just sustenance. Love to you both.

The fans of insanewiches.com: Hey, don't think for even one second I could forget all of you! What can I say? You're all insanely awesome—big time! Thanks for visiting my site daily, for your hilarious comments, and for making this book a reality.

contents

The First Slice

"Did you guys see that crazy sandwich pic forwarded this morning?" asks my lunchmate, forming an imaginary square with her fingers in mid-air. "It had different cubes of meat and cheese in it—man, I just wanted to take a bite out of the screen!"

I'm eating with friends. They're going on about an e-mail that bounced around the office that morning. The picture attached was a bizarre-looking sandwich resembling a Rubik's Cube. They're clueless at this point that the subject of their conversation is the product of my secret hobby, insanewiches.com, and that I'm the architect of that "crazy" sandwich. While they talk, I'm dying inside laughing, nearly choking on my food. I ask myself if I should spill the beans. Nah, why bother. I'm relishing anonymity way too much! As they continue, I think to myself: That sandwich is really making the old viral rounds, and now it's infiltrated my very own lunch table!

In late July, 2009, the blogosphere started buzzing. The food sites and geek blogs discovered my puzzling sandwich containing cubes of pastrami, kielbasa, pork fat, salami, and two types of cheddar. It was tagged by Serious Eats, made the front page of Digg.com, and was later featured in Gizmodo's *"10 Meat Structures That Require Engineering Degrees to Build and a Death Wish to Eat."* (Yeah, I busted a gut when I got that Google Alert.) Heck, the sandwich even went on to make the pages of Newsweek.com. The Rubik's Cubewich was discovered and it opened a portal into a land of "insane sandwich fun."

So you're probably wondering why anyone would create a blog (and book) about bizarre sandwiches. 'Cuz, at some point, lunch got boring, that's why! Take a look around you. People reach for run-of-the-mill ingredients—ham, cheese, lettuce, tomato—thoughtlessly slap them between two slices of bread and call it lunch. (Yawn.) It doesn't need to be this way. With a little inspiration and my easy-to-follow instructions, you'll be whipping up funky, far-out sandwiches in a snap.

In this book, I'll show you how to think outside the lunchbox. I'll give you simple instructions for 101 awesome insanewiches that will absolutely kick your boring lunch to the curb! I'll break down the must-have utensils you'll need within arm's reach to build your loony 'wiches. I call these implements the Instruments of Insanity and they're the tools you can't do without. One example is edible markers, which work like magic markers but leave results you can eat (see resource list at end of book). After I introduce you to the Instruments of Insanity, I'll provide the techniques to follow if you want to create a wacky 'wich. These are The Unique Techniques for Building an Insanewich. And on top of that, you'll find a special icon accompanying select recipes to indicate which sandwiches are kid-friendly.

Yesiree, it will be unavoidable: Your brother, aunt, boyfriend or girlfriend, husband or wife, best buddy, child, mom or dad will look at you like you've sprouted a second head when you show off the kooky creations from this book. But that's OK, because it's finally time to rethink lunch. It's time to turn lunch on its head! But before all that, let's figure out what it means to be an insanewich.

What the Heck is an Insanewich, Anyway?

Is your sandwich certifiably cuckoo? Not sure? Before your sandwich can be considered a true whack jobwich and before you diagnose it as insane, it's gotta possess one or more of the crazy criteria below.

It's gut-bustingly funny: I've actually watched friends and family LOL while surfing insanewiches.com or after I've slapped together one of my creations. The insanewiches you create at home will elicit the same response. Just think of the implications: She's had a rotten day and walks in the door oozing stress. Now, imagine the look on her face when she sees the *Luxury Vacation 'Wich* (page 107) you made just for her. You're sure to earn some brownie points (wink).

It's architecturally interesting or perplexing: Egyptian pyramids. Boring. Easter Island. Yawn. Stonehenge. Eyes getting heavy…Zzzzzzz. If you really wanna get your friends and family to wonder "How'd you do that?", present them with bizarre feats of sandwich engineering: you'll be the only one who knows how simple they are to construct.

It's a sandwich masquerading as…: No object is safe. Cell phones *and* cordless power drills are all fair game when gathering inspiration for insanewiches. Many of the selections from this book are loony because they're a spitting image of some real-world object. I mean, chances are you've never laid eyes upon a tie-shaped sandwich or a sandwich that looks like a digital camera!

It's got a mighty clever name: I know it sounds weird, but giving your sandwich a name that's punny—plays on words or is just plain funny—will accomplish three things. It'll make: 1) you and/or your sandwich recipient laugh even harder, 2) you seem smarter, and 3) your sandwich taste better.*

Disclaimer: Of course, I have no valid statistical data to back number three. Only the expressions on people's faces and the deliriously happy comments they make when they sink their teeth into, say, *The Fight Club* (page 78) or *The Swine 'N' Cheese* (page 112). So please don't sue me for making false claims.

It turns bread on its head: Flour, water, egg, yeast. These are the four pillars to any great bread, right? Not always. If you wanna show everyone you're out to lunch, you're gonna have to think outside the breadbox once in a while. Potato, rice cakes, mushroom, and even squash, for example, can all stand in nicely for bread. Heck, you can even reverse roles and use meat as bread and bread as meat!

It's trendy and topical: Next time you're watching the evening news, channel or web surfing, reading your favorite blog, or flipping through the paper (does anyone still read the newspaper?), keep your senses on high alert. Hot news items and juicy bits of pop culture are rich in sandwich-making inspiration. Don't believe me? Check out *The Jersey Shore Lunch* on page 74.

It incorporates props or elements of craft: When I go to the drawing board on an insanewich, I often incorporate some crafty elements or props—especially non-food-related ones (disclaimer: please remove before eating). A bit of ribbon, a golf tee, a wooden spoon, or a well-placed fishing lure all enhance meaning and raise an eyebrow.

So there it is: everything you need to know to get your insanewiching vibe on. Now let's get 'er going!

getting
down to
bizwich

Before setting foot in the kitchen to create your insanewiches, there are a few things you'll need handy and some stuff you gotta know...

The Instruments of Insanity

Just like a mad scientist, you'll need the proper tools to concoct your nutty sandwiches. These utensils should be within arm's reach if you hope to exclaim, "It's alive. The sandwich is alive!" Just about every item I mention is probably already lurking in your kitchen drawers or cupboards. The ones that aren't can be found at your local supermarket or online at the sites I provide in the resource list at the end of the book.

No-Brainer Implements:

CUTLERY

Chef's Knife

For about 20 bucks (steer clear of dollar-store cutlery), you can get yourself a high-quality, stainless steel chef's knife that'll last ages. And make sure you keep it sharp, because contrary to what you may have thought, a sharp knife is waaaaay safer than a dull one. If you slice a tomato with a dull chef's knife, you might earn a new nickname: Stumpy.

Bread Knife

Last I checked, most sandwiches (not all) contained bread. Duh! A bread knife, then, is an indispensible tool in your insane sandwich-making arsenal. Bread knives are serrated, so you can't really sharpen them (Please don't try to use a sharpening stone). Find one with a sturdy handle and a moderately flexible blade for maneuverability.

Steak Knife

This is my single most important knife when it comes specifically to insane sandwich bread carving. As you'll learn, a good steak knife works best when you're cutting bread into shapes using a paper template. It offers superior control when etching out tight little curves and turning corners. I never go insanewiching without one.

Paring Knife

Whenever you have fine work that doesn't involve bread, and must be carried out with the hands of a surgeon, your paring knife is tops. Since a paring knife is not serrated like most steak knives, it works great for cutting deli meats and cheeses into shapes or numbers without leaving marks or tears.

UTENSILS & ESSENTIALS

Cutting Board

Unless you've got no qualms about ruining your countertop, get a good, sturdy cutting board. If you choose wood, make sure to get one that's at least ¾ inch thick to help prevent warping and splitting over time. If you go with plastic, try to find one that's not too flexible, in order to keep your cutting surface flat. I own one of each. I break out the plastic board for meats and poultry because it's easier to sanitize; the wood one I use for everything else.

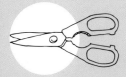

Kitchen Shears

A handy-dandy pair of kitchen shears is indispensible. They're mondo useful for cutting herbs right into a bowl, snipping a toothpick down to size, or even for cutting deli meat and cheese (see page 19)! And of course, I use my kitchen shears to cut out all of the paper templates I use.

Measuring Cups

Have on hand a tempered glass, 1-cup measuring cup for liquids and metal cups of varying sizes for dry ingredients. You may want to buy a 2-cup glass measuring cup for bigger projects.

Spatula

Ya ain't flippin' jack, Jack, if ya ain't got a spatula. Take special care when turning food over, especially if it's cooking in hot oil. I've seen people try to use a fork, or a spoon, or a fork and spoon. Honestly, it's awkward. The safest way is with the right spatula. I like the longer spatulas made from nonstick plastic. I find they offer better control and can be used in both nonstick and stainless steel pans.

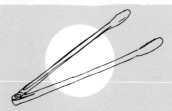

Tongs (Not thongs, that's another book. Not my book, someone else's.)

I have two pairs (one metal and one plastic) to accommodate almost any situation. I use the metal ones for stainless steel cookware and the plastic to avoid chipping my nonstick pan. A good pair of tongs is like an extension of your arm. You can easily pick up hot items or handle raw meat. And I use them for mixing salads and for stirring pasta when it's boiling in water.

Vegetable Peeler

Whenever I need long strips of vegetable (like carrot or cucumber), I use my vegetable peeler. I prefer a straight hand-held peeler with rubberized handle for a firm grip. This variety offers better control and safety, compared to Y-type peelers with a metal or hard plastic handle.

Cheese Grater

The obvious use for a cheese grater is, well, grating cheese. No surprises there. But it also comes in very handy when a recipe calls for room-temperature butter and all you've got is refrigerated or frozen. (Yeah, I routinely forget to take butter out of the fridge before I start cooking). In that case, just grate the cold butter right into the pan, pot, or bowl and it will soften in no time.

Whisk

When I'm motivated enough to make a made-from-scratch pancake batter, I always use a whisk to ensure the mixture is lump-free. Some commercial whisks can get pretty huge, but for the home cook, a hand-held kind that's between 10 and 12 inches long will do just fine.

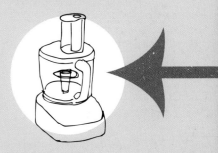

Food Processor

Yes, I am one of those crazy cooks who enjoys cutting stuff into a fine dice by hand. But when there just isn't the time, I break out the food processor. The one I own is a compact, 25-dollar countertop unit with one simple blade attachment and one speed. The container is 4 inches in diameter and almost 3 inches deep. It's ideal for making dressing, salsa, egg salads, and pestos. Since the recipes in this book don't require you to process large quantities or difficult-to-work-with ingredients, you won't need a processor that's big and fancy. But if you have one, great!

Strainer

True, they look like fencing masks, but they're also pretty useful when you gotta drain liquids or rinse veggies under the tap. A good, all-purpose-size strainer for sandwich making is about 7 or 8 inches in diameter. And a medium-fine mesh will do the trick for most kitchen tasks. Just make sure you wash yours immediately after use; otherwise food gets stuck in the mesh, which, quite frankly, is kinda nasty.

Colander

They're handy for draining pasta and for rinsing larger quantities of food. And here's a tip in case you don't have a strainer. Double-line the colander with some cheese cloth so that the holes won't allow smaller bits to pass through.

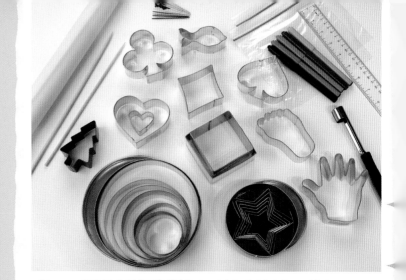

COOKWARE

Cast-Iron Skillet

A cast iron skillet is good for slapstick comedy, but it's also incredibly versatile in the kitchen. I use mine to sauté onions and make pancakes and frittatas, and I love that I can take it from stovetop to oven with no problems.

Cast-Iron Grill Pan

As the cast iron skillet's ridged cousin, the grill pan will allow you to cook meat and other items indoors, but still achieve that barbecue taste and char. Almost nothing's better than fixing a juicy seared steak with lovely grill marks on it in December. And it's a cinch to do: just heat the pan on your stovetop or in your oven using high heat, oil and grill away. Just remember, if you're in a smaller space, open some windows while you grill so you don't set off the fire alarm (yes, I learned that the hard way!).

Nonstick Fry Pan

Eggs, and grilled cheese almost always start off in my trusty nonstick. It's easy to clean and if you're cooking healthy, you can get away with using little oil. But never use metal utensils, 'cuz some of the coating could chip off and end up in your food. Sure, there are some brands that advertise "safe for use with metal implements," but I'm still skeptical.

Baking Sheet

Whenever I've got a bunch of smaller items or one fairly large, flat item to cook, I reach for the old baking sheet. The one I own is about 16 by 12 inches in size and has a nonstick coating. Just make sure not to use yours under the broiler, which could cause it to warp.

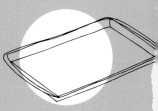

Sauce Pan and Stock Pot

Make sure they're stainless steel and heavy-bottomed to conduct heat evenly. Each should have its own lid and sturdy construction.

NOT-SO-OBVIOUS APPARATUSES

Assorted Cookie Cutters

Bread cuts just as easily (or easier) than cookie dough. Having an assortment of miscellaneous cookie cutters on hand (you name it, I've used it) will allow you to stamp out all sorts of funky bread shapes with zero effort. For your insanewiches, you'll need:

- A set of rounds (sizes ranging from 2 inches in diameter to 5½ inches)
- A set of stars (the smallest is roughly silver-dollar sized; the largest, the size of your palm)
- Two squares (2¾ inches and 3 inches, respectively)
- Large heart, small heart
- Club shape
- Diamond shape
- Spade shape
- Hand shape, foot shape
- Christmas tree shape
- Fish shape

Edible Markers

Need a really small ace of diamonds? Draw it in. Need to put dots on dice-shaped sandwiches? Scribe them on. With edible markers, getting that fine detail work done is a snap. They're available from cake supply companies, some major grocers, and online from the site recommended in my resource list.

Toothpicks and Skewers

When purchasing toothpicks, make sure they're decent quality. The last thing you want is a splinter left behind in your sandwich. And yes, size does matter, so use a toothpick that's the right length for the job. It's gotta be long enough to penetrate all the layers of bread, cheese, veg, and meat.

Edible Glues

Relax people, no one's asking you to down a tube of super glue. Many of the sandwiches in this book have little bits and pieces attached to them with mustard or decorating gel. And if these fail, you can always make a bit of homemade glue with one part water and one part flour (Remember your childhood papier maché-making days?).

Apple Corer

It's not just for apples, ya know. Whenever I need to make a small circle out of cheese, bread or meat, I can always count on my apple corer. You can stamp out several rounds in quick succession or just as easily make holes in an ingredient.

Parchment Paper

Several of the funky sandwich shapes and designs from this book start with a parchment paper template. Why parchment paper? It's real easy to trace shapes with because it's translucent, and it's a cinch to cut with kitchen shears. Find out how to make parchment paper templates on page 17.

Ruler

When it comes to making a perfectly straight line, I have no qualms about breaking out the old schoolhouse ruler. Buy one for sandwich making only and store it separately. You wouldn't want any pencil shavings or bits of eraser stuck to your cucumber.

Ziploc® Bags

Sometimes you'll need to pipe mayonnaise or mashed sweet potato onto a sandwich like it's vanilla frosting. In that case, a large Ziploc bag works as well as anything you'll find in an expensive cake supply store. I show you how to use a Ziploc bag for piping on page 18.

Shop 'Til Ya Dropwich!

As a sandwich maker on a mission, check these ingredients off your grocery list while you make a mad dash through the aisles.

FOR THE FRIDGE:

Mayonnaise

You can use it plain, sure. But mayonnaise is a great base for so many awesome flavors. Add lemon, dried chipotle or ancho chile powder, cumin, smoked paprika, curry powder, wasabi horseradish, regular horseradish, or minced garlic and you've got more than just plain-old mayo— you've got an über condiment that'll kick yer sammy up a notch!

ch.
1

015

Assorted Mustards

At any given time, you'll find no less than four different mustards in my fridge door. Today, for example, the selection includes: honey mustard, honey-Dijon, grainy, and, of course, yellow. The honey mustards offer a sweet contrast to sandwiches

containing salty meats and cheeses. The yellow adds a savory accent. Grainy mustard is great for providing texture. (I love it when those itty-bitty grains pop in my mouth!)

Salted Butter

The old saying, "Everything's better with butter", is pretty much true. If I'm not using olive oil, there's a pretty good chance you'll find butter somewhere in the recipe. It adds an unmistakable richness to sautéed onions or mushrooms and combines well with minced garlic. I say, if yer gonna have butter, have it and enjoy it.

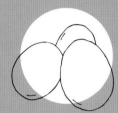

Eggs

Eggs are quite arguably the galaxy's most versatile food. Boiled, fried, scrambled—there are so many delicious incarnations. All cooks (crazy or sane) need this staple food in their fridge—unless, of course, they are allergic. If that's the case, stay the heck away from them.

Pickles

When I've completed an insanewich, I often enjoy it with a zesty pickle on the side. Many will disagree, but I actually consider pickles (maybe four or six of them at a time) a side dish. There I said it. I always have several kinds at the back of my fridge—kosher dills, half sours, and baby dills, to name a few.

Jams and Jellies

You'll notice a variety of jams and jellies inside the breakfast and dessert sandwiches—and maybe even in a savory sandwich (See *The Fool's Gold Loaf* on page 113). I never run low on my faves, which include pear, orange, blueberry, and grape.

FOR THE PANTRY:

Olive Oil

What can I say? I'm Italian! So I always gotta have olive oil close by. While the top-quality, cold-pressed, extra-virgin stuff isn't great for high-temperature frying (use canola or safflower oil, which has a higher smoke point), it sure works well for light sautés and most certainly in spreads or on salads.

Nut Butters

Peanut butter is great stuff, but don't feel like you have to limit yourself. Try other tasty nut butters, such as almond and cashew, to experiment with different flavors in your sweet insanewiches.

Food Coloring

I use food coloring in some pretty bizarre ways in this book. I manage to incorporate it with eggs, French toast, and even mayonnaise! When your sandwich needs some more visual appeal, food coloring is often the way to go.

Assorted Seasonings

Apart from salt and pepper, my go-to seasonings are ancho chile, chile powder, chipotle chile, cinnamon, cumin, curry powder, dry mustard, nutmeg, and paprika. I list them for you alphabetically because that's how they're arranged on my spice rack. Yes, I'm mildly OCD that way.

Decorating Gel

When I'm embellishing sweet sandwiches (See the hour hands on *The Donut Alarm Clock* on page 216), these handy little tubes of colored sugar and water make life real easy. Instead of cutting a feature out of food, I can just draw it on.

INSANEWICHES

016

The Unique Techniques for Building An Insanewich

Follow these tips and tricks as sandwich gospel. It's the only surefire way to end up with a weird 'wich and to show the world you've got a couple of loose screws!

BREAD CARVING WITH TEMPLATES

While flipping through the pages of this book at the bookstore (by the way, thanks for buying it!), you no doubt wondered how the heck you're gonna make some of these crazy sandwich shapes. Not to worry, the work's already done for you. By using the templates that accompany several of the recipes, you can carve out crazy bread shapes in a snap. Here's the process:

1. Place parchment paper over the pre-made template.

2. Trace the template using an edible marker.

3. Cut the template out with kitchen shears.

4. Stack the slices of bread on a cutting board and place the template on top. ***NOTE:*** *If you find that the parchment paper you're using flips or curls up (which would make it awkward to carve the shape), simply retrace the parchment paper cutout onto a regular sheet of white paper, cut that template out and use the white paper shape instead. This is the extra step I took to demonstrate this technique.*

5. Holding your steak knife vertically, cut into the bread crust until you reach the template.

6. Follow the template using a very small sawing motion with the steak knife until you've reached the starting point.

7. Pull away the excess bread and the shape is complete.

Tips:

- Do not move the sandwich when you need to turn a sharp corner with the knife; instead, move the entire cutting board.

- Hold the paper template with your non-cutting hand if it begins to shift.

You can use this same technique to carve shapes out of cheese, thicker slices of meat, potato or almost anything else you use as "bread." But in those cases, use a paring knife instead of a steak knife (which is serrated) to avoid tearing and shredding.

CUTTING BREAD WITH A COOKIE CUTTER

Sometimes you won't need a template if the sandwich design is based on shapes that can be formed with a cookie cutter. Here's how to properly execute:

1. Place the bread slice on a cutting board and center the cookie cutter on the slice of bread.

2. In one motion, press firmly using the whole palm of your hand.

3. When you've hit the chopping board, slightly wriggle the cutter to ensure the bread is cut through and the shape is completely free.

4. Gently release the shape from the cutter using your fingers.

Tips:

- Try to avoid cutting into the crust unless the recipe directs you to do so.

- Avoid pressing down on the cookie cutter with your fingers because you may put too much pressure on one side and end up with an uneven, lopsided slice.

- You can use this technique with one or more slices of bread.

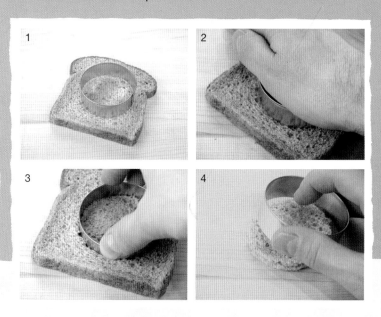

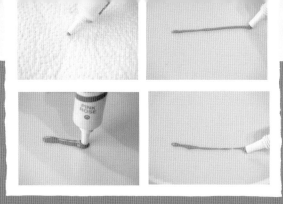

SANDWICH ARTISTRY WITH EDIBLE MARKERS

Draw on my sandwich? It sounds nuts, I know, but cake decorators draw on cakes all the time, so who says a sandwich maker can't? And it's easy, too.

Tips:

- When drawing a dot, hold the marker as vertically as you can, working the small circle out from the middle.

- When etching a line freehand, hold the marker at about a 45-degree angle to minimize bleeding of the ink. Remember, peeps, this is foodstuff, so it's fairly porous.

- If you're filling in a shape, you can hold the marker more horizontally to cover more area quicker.

Warning:

The only part of an edible marker that's actually edible is the ink left on the sandwich, not the marker itself, which is made from plastic…which would taste horrible. Yes, even if it were wrapped in bacon. Just don't eat the markers, all right?

FEARLESS FROSTING

Store-bought decorating gels provide an easy way to add design elements to your dessert sandwich. My trick is to stick them in the fridge about 15 minutes before I start so I'm not using them at room temperature. I find colder gel is easier to work with and much less likely to shoot out of the tube uncontrollably (I've had to redo a few sandwiches due to unwanted gel snake attacks!). Refrigerated gel also won't trail off or smudge as easily.

Tips:

- After removing the gel from the fridge, squeeze a tiny bit out on a tester area like a paper towel. Often, the sugar and water will separate at the tip of the tube when not in use.

- When drawing lines, keep the tube tilted at about a 45-degree angle.

- Don't draw with the tube completely vertical. The lines could end up too thick and wobbly.

- Avoid tilting the tube too far horizontally or you could experience trailing and smudging.

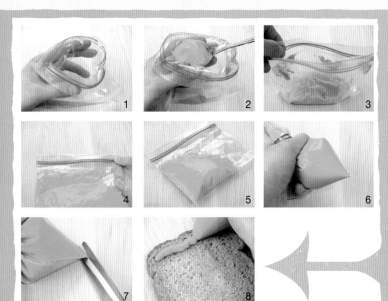

PERFECT PIPING PRACTICES

Specialty piping bags are fine, but if you want more bang for your buck, grab some Ziploc bags next time you're grocery shopping. And whether you're using the larger freezer-sized variety or smaller sandwich bags, the drill for piping is pretty much the same:

1. Turn the top zipper-locking portion of the bag over your hand.

2. Spoon in the filling.

3. Turn the zipper-locking portion back up.

4. Squeeze as much air out of the bag as you can and seal the top.

5. Squeeze the contents of the bag into one corner.

6. Twist the top of the bag and keep it firmly in your hand.

7. Cut a ¼- to ½-inch tip from the filled corner.

8. Using a slow and steady motion, pipe the ingredient.

CUTTING DELI MEAT USING SHEARS

When it comes to cold cuts, sometimes there's overhang, and the meat needs to be trimmed to fit. Enter your faithful kitchen shears. I know what you're thinking: cutting through sliced turkey breast like it's construction paper is weird. You'll get used to it real quick. Most kitchen shears are dishwasher safe too, so don't worry about contamination.

Tips:

- When cutting, follow the shape of the template with the shears to ensure accuracy.
- If necessary, hold the cold cut in place with your non-cutting hand to increase stability and to keep the meat's edges from fraying.

SKINNING BELL PEPPERS

Bell peppers are ideal for adding colorful accents to your insanewich. But when you open them up, you'll find the skin is thick, which makes them hard to work with. For this reason, you'll have to skin them alive. Relax…you won't hear shrieks of terror if you apply these skinning techniques:

1. With a chef's knife, cut around the core of the pepper four times and discard the core. Wash off any seeds from the flesh and the knife. You should have four segments.

2. Cut the ends of each segment.

3. With the knife, make an incision right above the outer skin.

4. Then carefully slide the knife until the outer layer of skin has separated.

5. You now have a paper-thin piece of pepper that you can readily cut into little strips or stamp into shapes.

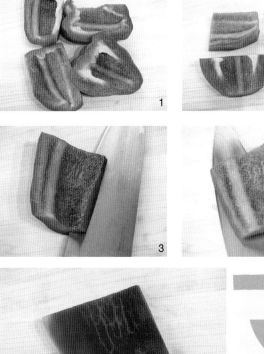

sunrise
wiches

Rise 'n' shine, sleepyhead! 'Cuz the day is calling and so are the Sunrisewiches. Whether you've slept in (lucky you) or been jolted awake by your blasted alarm, start your day off on the right foot with these a.m. insanewiches.

Pancake Popwiches

Who could possibly resist brekkie on a stick? Especially when peanut butter and hazelnut-chocolate spread are sandwiched between hot 'n' buttery pancakes. How would *you* eat 'em? Would you pick them up gingerly, admire how cutelicious they look then nibble slowly? Or would you stick them in your mouth, bite down, and...om nom nom nom!

You'll Need:

2 medium-sized pancakes (5-inch diameter)*

2 tablespoons Nutella®

2 tablespoons peanut butter

1 teaspoon butter (very small pat)

Instruments:

Toaster, 1 round cookie cutter (2½ inches in diameter), 2 large skewers, 1 medium-sized baking sheet, 1 piece of tin foil (about 12 X 12 inches).

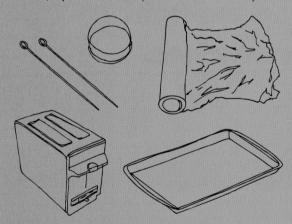

Assembly:

1. Toast store-bought pancakes or make homemade. (See page 45 for homemade recipe.)

2. With your cookie cutter, stamp out two rounds from each pancake: four total.

3. Spread 1 tablespoon of Nutella and 1 tablespoon of peanut butter on one round. Repeat on a second round.

4. Top each round containing filling with the remaining two rounds.

5. Insert one skewer into the side of each little sandwich. Only insert it about 1½ inches, making sure it doesn't poke out the other side.

6. Next, place a tiny pat of butter on top of one popwich. Optional: place another pat on the second popwich.

7. Place both popwiches on the baking sheet and freeze overnight.

8. The next morning, preheat your oven to 300°F.

9. Remove the popwiches from the freezer and cover the skewers with tin foil so they won't burn.

10. Place the tray in the oven for 1–3 minutes, or until the butter starts to melt. Remove and serve.

11. The popwiches will still be semi-frozen, but that's the best way to eat them!

*I confess, I used store-bought pancakes and waffles for several of these breakfast insanewiches. I find their uniform size and texture a cinch to work with. And they taste just as good as homemade if you buy a quality brand like Eggo®. But since I can hear y'all giving me the old "tsk, tsk, shame on you!" loud and clear, I've included a recipe for my fave made-from-scratch pancake and waffle mix on page 45.

The Laid-Back Hamcake

Meet the Mr. Rogers of sandwiches. No kidding, it's one of the most relaxed breakfast sandwiches you can make. All you have to do is stack a few ingredients, pour the syrup and watch it flow over the edge. It's perfect for those mornings you feel so mellow that you just can't get outta your PJs.

You'll Need:

- **2** medium-sized pancakes
- **1** tablespoon butter
- **2** slices maple-cured ham
- **1** slice Swiss cheese
- **6–8** blueberries
- **2–3** tablespoons maple syrup

Instruments:

Toaster, 1 toothpick

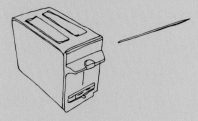

Assembly:

1. Toast store-bought pancakes or make homemade. (See page 45 for homemade recipe.)
2. Spread butter on one pancake.
3. Lay the slices of maple-cured ham on buttered pancake, folding them in half.
4. Lay the slice of Swiss cheese on the ham and top the sandwich with the second pancake.
5. Stab the toothpick through the top of the sandwich to keep everything in place and then impale one blueberry on the toothpick.
6. Scatter the remaining blueberries around the sandwich and drizzle the maple syrup over the top.

A sandwich that likes to go with the flow!

➤➤ *It's OK to make a split decision.*

The In-Betweener

A lotta diners serve the classic waffle 'n' egg breakfast and grilled cheese lunch. But my guess is you'll never come across a dish that combines the two. Enter The In-Betweener. With golden waffles, two types of syrup, processed cheese, and one egg fried sunny-side up, it may seem indecisive, but it's still delish!

You'll Need:

2	waffles
2	slices processed cheese
3	tablespoons butter
1	egg
2–3	tablespoons chocolate syrup
2–3	tablespoons strawberry syrup

Instruments:

Toaster, 1 medium-sized skillet, 1 spatula

Assembly:

1. Toast store-bought waffles or make homemade (see page 45 for homemade recipe).

2. Place two slices of processed cheese on top of one waffle and top with the other.

3. Put 2 tablespoons of butter in skillet over medium heat. When butter is melted, place sandwich in skillet.

4. With your spatula, flip the sandwich after about 3–4 minutes or when the cheese starts to melt.

5. Grill the second side for another 3–4 minutes or until golden.

6. Remove the sandwich from the pan and cut in half to reveal its gooey contents. Place on dish.

7. In the same skillet, add remaining butter. Fry egg sunny-side up (or however you prefer). Place in dish next to sandwich.

8. Squeeze chocolate and strawberry syrup into alternating squares on top of the sandwich to achieve the checkered effect.

The Breakfast Club

Warning: This behemoth's got layers of bacon, lettuce, turkey, and cheese between four—count 'em—four waffles. It may cause drowsiness. Do not operate heavy equipment after use. Calorie-sensitive individuals may experience that weighed-down feeling for the remainder of the day. Do not combine with other crazy 'wiches. Do not exceed one sandwich per day.

You'll Need:

- **4** waffles
- **3** Boston lettuce leaves (washed and dried)
- **6** slices tomato (large)
- **6** slices oven-roasted turkey breast
- **9** slices bacon
- **3** slices cheddar
- **1** scoop vanilla ice cream
- **1** olive
- **3** tablespoons maple syrup
- **1** small bag of chips
- **2** tablespoons mayonnaise

Instruments:

Toaster, chef's knife, nonstick skillet, ice cream scooper, 1 large skewer

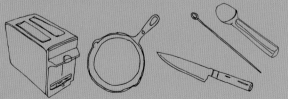

> ➤ *Please eat this sandwich only as directed.*

Assembly:

1. Toast store-bought waffles or make homemade. (See page 45 for homemade recipe.)

2. On top of the first waffle, stack 1 Boston lettuce leaf, 2 slices of tomato, 2 slices of turkey breast (each folded in half), 3 slices of bacon, and 1 slice of cheddar. Place the next waffle on top.

3. Repeat Step 2 two more times to achieve three layers in total.

4. Place a scoop of vanilla ice cream on top of the sandwich.

5. Pierce the skewer through the ice cream scoop and all layers of the structure. Make sure the pointy end is facing up.

6. Impale the olive on top of the skewer and then drizzle the sandwich with syrup 'til it runs down the sides.

7. Serve with chips and mayo on the side.

Toad in the Hole in One

We all know you're not going to tee off from the sandwich, but you gotta admit, it'll make a pretty solid starter before going out and hitting the links. And you'll need one too because playing 9 holes takes a while—especially if you're prone to the odd triple bogey!

You'll Need:

2 slices whole wheat bread

2 tablespoons butter

1 egg

2 slices provolone cheese

2 slices of prosciutto

Instruments:

1 round cookie cutter (2½ inches in diameter), cast-iron skillet, 1 spatula, clean golf tee, clean golf ball

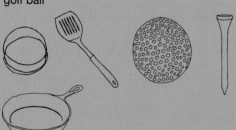

Assembly:

1. Make a hole in one slice of bread with cookie cutter, placing it in the upper left corner of the slice.

2. Melt 1 tablespoon butter in a cast-iron skillet over medium-low heat.

3. Brown the non-hole slice in skillet for 2–3 minutes per side or until golden. Set aside.

4. Melt remaining butter in skillet and brown the holed slice for 2–3 minutes on one side or until golden.

5. After flipping the holed slice with spatula, crack egg and gently aim it into the hole. Fry for 3–4 minutes or until the white has set. You can flip the bread slice again if you prefer your egg over easy. Remove slice from pan with spatula and set aside.

6. On top of the non-hole slice, layer the cheese and then the slices of prosciutto, each folded.

7. Using the spatula, carefully top the sandwich with the holed slice.

8. Stick the golf tee into the sandwich beside the hole and the ball on the tee.

Eggo-ticons

There are two camps in life: Those who use emoticons in texts and e-mail :) and those who hate people who use emoticons in texts and e-mail :(If you fall into the latter category, try not to get annoyed with me for making these Eggo-emoticon sandwiches. After all, they create some pretty delightful emotions after you eat them. And I just thought you could use a little cheering up this early in the morning ;).

Surprised Eggo-ticon

You'll Need:

- **2** waffles
- **3** tablespoons ricotta cheese
- **1** tablespoon honey
- **2** sour strings (2 inches long)
- **2** green jujubes
- **1** black jujube
- **1** sour peach ring

Instruments:

Saucepan, nonstick skillet, toaster, chef's knife

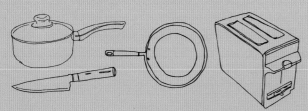

Assembly:

1. Toast store-bought waffles or make homemade. (See page 45 for homemade recipe.)
2. Spread ricotta cheese on one waffle and drizzle honey over top of ricotta.
3. Top with second waffle.
4. Use sour strings as eyebrows (make sure they're slanted to look surprised).
5. Use green jujubes as eyes and black one as nose.
6. Use sour peach ring as mouth.

Happy Eggo-ticon

You'll Need:

- **1** egg
- **1** breakfast sausage
- **2** waffles
- **1** slice Havarti cheese
- **3** slices bacon, fried crisp
- **1** small pimento olive
- **1** large pimento olive

continued ➔

Did you ask for a sandwich
or a sand wedge?

Assembly:

1. In a saucepan, hard-boil egg for 6–8 minutes, drain water, cool and peel.

2. Bend a raw breakfast sausage into a smile and cook so it will retain that shape.

3. Toast store-bought waffles or make homemade. (See page 45 for homemade recipe.)

4. Place slice of Havarti cheese on top of one waffle and the bacon on top of the cheese. Top with second waffle.

5. Slice two cross sections from hard-boiled egg. Place on top as eyes.

6. Slice two cross sections of small pimento olive and use as eye pupils.

7. Slice one cross section from large pimento olive and use as nose.

8. Use sausage to create mouth.

Hey, leggo my personified breakfast sandwich!

Bowl of Cerealwich

If you love cereal first thing in the morning, you can still enjoy an insanewich: Introducing the new Insanewiches™ brand cereal sandwich. It's high in flipped-out fiber and provides nine nutty nutrients in every serving. This wholesome and fruit loopy breakfast cerealwich also contains omega-3 freaky acids, which assist in the maintenance of mental well-being.* Now, you and your family will enjoy the taste that craziness brings every morning!

Disclaimer: This is a joke, of course. I have no way to verify any of this.

You'll Need:

- **3** shredded wheat rounds
- **4** tablespoons yogurt (I like strawberry)
- **1** tablespoon strand fiber cereal (Kellogg's® All-Bran®)
- **2** ounces Froot Loops®
- **2** ounces assorted nuts: cashews, walnuts, and almonds
- **2** ounces assorted berries (cleaned and washed): strawberries, blueberries, blackberries, red and yellow raspberries
- **1** cup milk

Assembly:

1. Place first shredded wheat round in bowl and spoon 2 tablespoons of yogurt over top.
2. Place the second shredded wheat round on top of the first and spoon remaining yogurt on top.
3. Place the third shredded wheat round on top and arrange the face: strand fiber cereal for hair, Froot Loop eyes, ½ cut strawberry as nose, and a cashew smile.
4. Add remaining berries, nuts and Froot Loops around the side of the bowl and pour in milk.

Instruments:

Bowl

Stop The Madwich

Here's a sandwich that'll help with work stress. When you've got a report due by nine, an exec presentation at ten, and a pile of papers on your desk that's two feet high, you can vent your frustrations before getting to the office by pounding out ingredients for this sandwich. You'll be glad you did.

You'll Need:

- **2** tablespoons butter, cut into two ½-inch-thick squares
- **4** ounces walnuts
- **½** banana
- **2** crumpets (if you can't find crumpets use English muffins)
- **2** tablespoons mascarpone cheese
- **2** raisins

Instruments:

Chef's knife, chopping board, apple corer, 2 Ziploc bags, toaster, spoon, steak knife

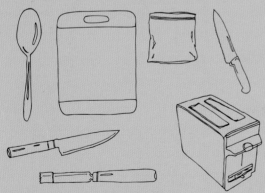

Assembly:

1. Cut two ½-inch-thick squares from a refrigerated stick of butter. Place the squares on a chopping board and use the apple corer to stamp out a small round from each.

2. Place the rounds on a small plate and refrigerate for at least 15 minutes.

3. Place walnuts in a Ziploc bag, reserving half of one walnut. Remove as much air as possible from the bag and seal. Pulverize nuts with your fist until they are smashed into small bits.

4. Place banana in Ziploc bag. Remove as much air as possible and seal. Smash banana into a paste with your fist.

5. Toast one crumpet for 2–3 minutes or until golden and spread with mascarpone cheese.

6. Remove banana from bag with a spoon and spread on top of mascarpone, then remove walnuts from bag and sprinkle on top of banana.

7. Using a steak knife, cut a zig-zag shape for a mouth out of the second crumpet.

8. Toast both pieces of the second crumpet for 2–3 minutes or until golden.

9. Immediately after they pop out of the toaster, use them to top the sandwich.

10. While the crumpet is still hot, remove the butter rounds from the fridge and place on top of the sandwich to form the eyes. Place one raisin pupil on each butter eye.

11. With your steak knife, cut the reserved walnut half in two and place the pieces above the butter eyes on a slant to create a disgruntled expression.

2
035

Don't get angry, get eating!

Step 3

Step 7

Married Sausages

If these breakfast sausages were a married couple trying to get some sleep, here's what they'd say:

Mrs. Sausage: For the last time, hun, quit hogging the omelet! I'm freezing here!

Mr. Sausage: Stop complaining. Every time *you* roll over, you hit my casing!

Mrs. Sausage: Well, if you didn't sizzle so loudly all night, I might not be so restless.

Mr. Sausage: That's it! I've had it! I'm going to sleep out on the skillet.

You'll Need:

- **3** slices of bread (the largest you can find)
- **2** large breakfast sausages
- **2** slices Canadian bacon
- **2** eggs
- **2** tablespoons milk
- **2** slices Monterey Jack cheese
- **2** toothpicks

Instruments:

Cast iron skillet, tin foil (12 X 12 inches), small bowl, fork, spatula, 3-inch square cookie cutter, 2 toothpicks

Assembly:

1. Using the templates provided for this recipe, and the bread-carving technique described on page 17, cut out the bread shapes required for this sandwich (2 leg pieces, box spring and mattress, and headboard). Set aside.

2. Preheat oven to 250°F.

3. In a cast iron skillet over medium heat, cook the breakfast sausages and Canadian bacon. Wrap in foil and place in preheated oven to keep warm. Leave skillet on oven range and turn heat to medium low.

4. In a small bowl, mix together eggs and milk with a fork. Pour mixture into skillet. You won't need to add extra oil because there will be leftover fat in the skillet from the sausage and bacon.

5. Cook egg mixture for 2–3 minutes and flip using a spatula. Cook the other side for 2 minutes. Be careful not to fold it! You want it as flat as possible.

6. Turn off oven range and remove the skillet from the heat, but leave eggs in pan to keep warm. The skillet will retain heat for a while.

7. Toast the box spring, mattress, and headboard. Don't bother with the legs. They're too small.

8. Place the legs on a plate parallel to each other, 5 inches apart.

9. Set the box spring on top of the legs and place the cheese on the box spring.

continued ➤

10. Remove sausages and bacon from the oven and place the bacon on the cheese.

11. Cover with the mattress and place two sausages on top of the mattress.

12. Remove egg from skillet using a spatula and place omelet on a chopping board.

13. Using the square cookie cutter, stamp out the egg blanket and cover the sausages.

14. Affix the headboard, using toothpicks from behind. Make sure they stick securely into the mattress bread slice, and don't forget to remove them before eating.

Step 14

TEMPLATES

Legs

Headboard

**Box Spring
and Mattress**

The French Toast Flagwich

The French offer some pretty tasty foods, such as chevre and French toast. So to pay tribute, I combine the two in a French flag-shaped sandwich, which is sure to be talked about by beret-wearing existentialists who smoke and commiserate at small street-side cafés.

You'll Need:

- **2** slices white bread
- **8½** ounces (approx.) carton liquid egg whites
- **15–20** drops blue food coloring
- **15–20** drops red food coloring
- **2** tablespoons butter
- **3** tablespoons goat cheese
- **2** tablespoons apricot preserves

Instruments:

Bread knife, three bowls, cast iron skillet, slotted spoon, spatula

Assembly:

1. Using a bread knife, cut the crusts from two stacked slices of bread so they both create even rectangles that measure about 5 by 3 inches.

2. Set one slice aside and cut the other into three even pieces widthwise. Set aside.

3. Divide the carton of egg whites into roughly three equal portions pouring into three separate bowls.

4. Add blue color to one bowl and red to another. Don't add color to the last bowl. Using a separate fork for each color, incorporate the blue and red food color into the egg whites in their respective bowls.

5. Melt 1 tablespoon butter in a cast iron skillet over medium low heat.

6. Take one of the ⅓-slice bread pieces and place it in the blue mixture. Place the second piece in the red mixture, and the third in the non-colored mixture. Submerge each for only 5 seconds.

7. Remove each piece with a slotted spoon, draining off any excess, and place them all in skillet.*

8. Panfry each side of each piece for about 1–2 minutes. Remove them from skillet with spatula and set aside.

9. Melt the remaining butter in skillet over medium low heat.

* Tips to avoid color mixing: 1) give the slotted spoon a quick rinse before removing each section from its respective egg mixes, 2) keep the pieces as far apart as possible in the skillet while cooking.

continued ➤➤

10. Submerge the bread slice that wasn't divided in the remaining non-colored egg white. Panfry each side for 1–2 minutes. Remove from skillet with spatula and place on plate.

11. Spread it with goat cheese and then with apricot preserve. Arrange the thirds on top from left to right: blue, white, red.

Vive le French toast!

The Whatsamatta Frittata Sandwich

I'm sure a few wooden spoon-wielding Italian nonnas would scoff at the use of pre-packaged polenta in this sandwich. "Whatsa matta for you?" one of them would complain, threatening with the spoon, "Why you no mekka da polenta by hand, ah?" Nonna, it takes forever to make polenta! So please put down the spoon, and by God, don't get any crazy ideas with that rolling pin!

You'll Need:

4 eggs

¼ cup milk

salt and pepper to taste

4 slices pancetta

2½ tablespoons olive oil

3 tablespoons red onion, chopped

5 asparagus shoots, sliced

1 small zucchini, diced

½ orange bell pepper, diced

3 slices polenta, from premade tube (each ¾ inch thick)

Instruments:

Bowl, baking sheet, cast-iron skillet, grill pan, 1 round cookie cutter (3½ inch diameter), ¼-inch-thick skewer, 1 small wooden spoon

Assembly:

1. Preheat oven to 350°F.

2. In a Bowl, combine eggs, milk, salt, and pepper and mix thoroughly. Set aside.

3. Place slices of pancetta on a baking sheet and cook in oven for 7–8 minutes or until pancetta is crisp. Remove from oven and set aside. Leave oven on.

4. Add 1½ tablespoons olive oil to a cast-iron skillet over medium heat. Add red onion, asparagus, zucchini, orange bell pepper to skillet and sauté for 4–5 minutes or until veggies are soft.

5. Add egg mixture to skillet and cook on stovetop for 4–5 minutes, then place in oven for another 10–15 minutes or until all the egg has set. Remove skillet from oven and allow the frittata to cool down.

6. Slice the three slices of polenta. Each should be about ¾ inch thick.

7. Drizzle both sides of each polenta slice with remaining olive oil and place on a grill pan over high heat. Grill each side of each slice for 4–5 minutes to achieve the perfect grill marks.

8. Using round cookie cutter, stamp out two disks from the frittata. Each should be about ¾ inch thick.

9. Stack as follows: one polenta slice, two slices of pancetta, one frittata round, the next polenta slice, two slices of pancetta, the second frittata round, and the final slice of polenta.

continued ➤➤

> ➤ **There'll be hell to pay if Nonna finds out
> it's not ALL homemade!** ◄

10. Poke a hole down through the center of the structure with the skewer. This will allow the spoon to slide in easily.

11. Remove the skewer and carefully slide the wooden spoon handle down into the hole.

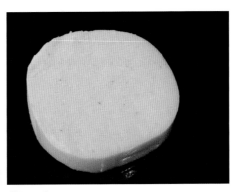

Step 6

Step 8

Great for
● Kids!

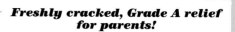
➤ *Freshly cracked, Grade A relief for parents!*

The Good Eggwich

Getting your kids outta bed can be a Herculean task some mornings, right? Just think how fast the kids will spring out from under the covers when they know The Good Eggwich is waiting at the table with a big sunny-side up smile. That's right; now you have the perfect before-school bargaining chip for those challenging days.

You'll Need:

- **1** slice whole wheat or white bread
- **1** teaspoon olive oil
- **1** egg
- **1** slice processed cheese
- **¼** inch-thick slice of salami
- **2** squirts of ketchup

Instruments:

Nonstick pan, chopping board, 1 round cookie cutter (4 inches in diameter), steak knife

Assembly:

1. Lightly toast bread.

2. Add olive oil to nonstick pan over medium heat and fry egg sunny side up. Spread the whites of the egg by tipping the pan from side to side and front and back. It will take about 4–5 minutes for the whites to set.

3. Remove egg from pan and place on the chopping board.

4. With round cookie cutter, stamp out a circle from the egg whites, keeping the yolk centered within the cutter.

5. Place the slice of cheese on the toast and place the egg on the cheese.

6. Cut the salami slice in half. It will resemble a half moon. Then using a steak knife, carve the center out from one of these halves to form a smiley mouth.

7. Place the salami smile below the yolk, and squirt two dabs of ketchup above the yolk as eyes.

*Perfect Pancakes and Waffles For 'Wiches

When it comes to breakfast sandwiches, I'm so over English muffins. Try mixing things up by stuffing your breakfast fillings between a coupla pancakes or waffles. Here's a no-fail, made-from-scratch pancake and waffle recipe that works every time! An über-heavy cast iron skillet is tops for this job, but a medium-sized nonstick pan will work fine too. And remember, if you're gonna be stamping any shapes outta these homemade pancakes, let 'em cool a bit first so they won't fall apart.

You'll Need:

DRY INGREDIENTS

2 cups all-purpose flour

¼ cup sugar

1 teaspoon baking powder

¼ teaspoon salt

WET INGREDIENTS

1 egg

¾ cup milk

1 tablespoon crème fraîche

1 tablespoon sour cream

¼ teaspoon vanilla extract

½ tablespoon butter per pancake

Instruments:

Mixing bowl, whisk, cast-iron skillet or waffle iron, large ladle, spatula

Assembly:

1. Combine all dry ingredients in a large mixing bowl. Whisk thoroughly to incorporate.

2. Add egg, milk, crème fraîche, sour cream, and vanilla.

3. Mix with whisk until batter is smooth.

4. Melt ½ tablespoon of butter in pan over medium-low heat.

5. Pour ⅓-cup ladle of batter onto pan (or preheated, nonstick waffle iron).

6. After about 3 minutes, flip pancake with spatula and cook on other side for 3 minutes. Remove.

7. Repeat steps 4–6 until batter is gone.

game
wiches

3

Everyone needs a little downtime, right? That's why there's one insanewich breed that's especially mouthwatering for procrastinators, distraction-seekers, and those trying to escape the clutches of boredom. These Gamewiches sneakily distract us from seriousness and interfere with schoolwork, laundry, and book writing (oops, meant to think that!). Yep, there's a 'wich here with your fave leisure activity's name on it.

➤ *Sammy's got a checkered past.* ◄

King Me

The Ham-and-Cheese Checkerboard

This insanewich is based on the classic board game, which conjures up images of rainy days at the cottage when you're swaddled in a blanket by the fire... and getting drubbed three times in a row by your older sister! Ouch! I hope this sandwich version won't stir up such painful memories.

You'll Need:

- **3** slices of yellow cheddar cheese
- **2** large slices of white bread (the biggest you can find!)
- **5** slices of maple-cured ham
- **2** slices of bologna
- mustard
- **1** slice of white cheddar cheese

Instruments:

Chef's knife, cutting board, apple corer

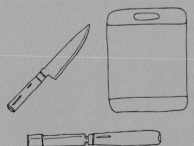

Assembly:

1. Lay two of the yellow slices of cheddar on one slice of bread and then neatly arrange the five slices of maple ham over the cheese, carefully folding each slice of ham in half. Place the second slice of bread on top.

2. With your knife, cut the two slices of bologna into several ¾-inch squares. How many you cut will depend on the size of your bread. My bread slices were big, so I had to use 18 squares.

3. Lay the bologna squares over the top slice of bread in a checkered pattern, using a small dab of mustard under each as adhesive.

4. With the apple corer, stamp out several small rounds from the remaining white and yellow cheddar slices. Place them randomly on top of the checkerboard to mimic a game in progress.

5. Make sure to double up on some of the pieces that have made it to the opposing player's side. Those ones have been kinged!

Sandwich Dominoes

Competitors often slap dominoes down emphatically when they're lining up the dots. "Take that!" they'll say, harshly rubbing it in. But if they tried the same with these Sandwich Dominoes, they'd just end up with a smooshed sandwich. When eaten as a snack, this finger food fills in the hunger gap quite nicely between games.

You'll Need:

2 small sandwich wraps

1 tablespoon prepared horseradish

1 slice of roast beef (have it cut thick at your deli counter)

1 large slice of Swiss cheese

1 romaine lettuce leaf, washed and dried

Instruments:

Cutting board, 2¾-inch square cookie cutter, chef's knife, black edible marker

Assembly:

1. Lay the first sandwich wrap on the cutting board, and slather it with horseradish.

2. Next, lay the roast beef, Swiss cheese, and romaine lettuce on top of the first wrap and top all ingredients with the second wrap.

3. Place the cookie cutter on top of the second wrap.

4. Using the cookie cutter as a guide, carefully cut away the excess with your knife. You will be left with a square sandwich.

5. Cut this square in half to make two identical rectangles.

6. With your marker, draw a line centered along the width of each rectangle.

7. Lastly, draw the dots with your marker.

Experience the sandwich domino effect!

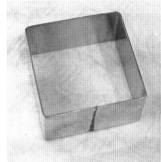

Step 3

Step 4

Step 6

A Pair of Turkey Club Acewiches

Maybe it's poker night at your place and friends are on their way. In that case, you'll need some cold drinks, tunes rockin' in the background, a stack of 52 and...hmm, what the heck are you going to feed these card sharks?...How about A Pair of Turkey Club Acewiches? These sammies boast everything turkey with some cool cucumber poker chips as well.

You'll Need:

- **4** large pieces of your favorite flatbread
- **2** tablespoons mayo
- **4** slices turkey breast deli meat
- **2** medium tomatoes, sliced
- **6** slices turkey bacon, fried crisp
- **2** tablespoons honey mustard
- **1** cucumber (7 inches long)

Instruments:

cutting board, chef's knife, waxed paper, kitchen shears, black and red edible markers, vegetable peeler

Assembly:

1. Lay the first flatbread slice on the cutting board and slather it with 1 tablespoon of mayo.

2. Stack two slices of turkey breast, one sliced tomato, and three slices of turkey bacon on the slathered slice.

3. Slather the second flatbread with 1 tablespoon honey mustard and use it to top the sandwich.

4. Using your chef's knife, cut the stacked items into a rectangle 3½ by 5 inches in size, using the template provided and the technique described on page 17.

5. With the remaining ingredients, repeat all the steps above to create the second Acewich.

6. Using waxed paper, trace the diamond and spade designs from the templates provided.

7. Cut out the diamond and spade from the waxed paper with your kitchen shears.

8. Place the diamond cutout on the center of one sandwich and trace it with the red edible marker.

9. Then fill in the outline with the same color.

10. On the other sandwich, repeat steps 8–9 with the spade, using the black marker.

continued ➤➤

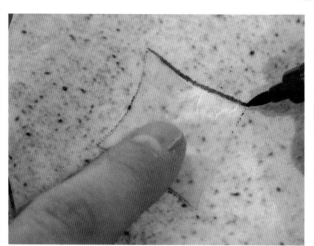
Step 8

Step 9

11. The little "A" and card suit on opposing corners are small enough, so draw them freehand.

12. Cut 1 inch off either side of the cucumber.

13. Using the vegetable peeler, peel a strip of skin from the cucumber, give it a one-third turn in your hand and peel another strip, give it another one-third turn and peel the last strip.

14. Cut the cucumber into ¼-inch slices and stack around each sandwich in three uneven piles to mimic poker chips.

❦ TEMPLATES ❦

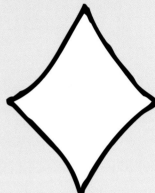

Spade and Diamond

Rectangle

The Rubik's Cubewich

We can't forget the insanewich that got the ball rolling. One commenter at insanewiches.com asks, "But can it be solved?" The answer, I think, is a resounding no! Unlike its plastic predecessor, the cold-cut-and-cheddar version was received with delight, disgust, and disbelief. Smithsonian.com called it "a truly horrifying concoction" and many others recoiled at the unabashed use of cubed pork fat. But there are those who've interpreted the sandwich in a completely different way. On seriouseats.com, somebody suggested that it would make a fun idea for a cheese tray. Even a vegetarian (a vegetarian!) loved the 80's kitsch.

You'll Need:

- **5** ounces pastrami (ask to have one slice cut ¾-inch thick at the deli counter)

- **5** ounces kielbasa

- **5** ounces pork belly (yes, pork belly. The Rubik's Cubewich needs white squares!)

- **5** ounces salami (buy a whole salami, not sliced)

- **4** ounces yellow cheddar (slab, not sliced)

- **3** ounces white cheddar (slab, not sliced)

- **2** slices of light rye bread

Assembly:

1. On the cutting board, cut each of the above meat and cheese items into ¾-inch cubes: five cubes of each meat, four cubes of yellow cheddar, three cubes of white cheddar. Set aside.

2. Toast the two slices of rye until golden. Place the real Rubik's Cube on top of each bread slice as a template and cut away the excess with your knife.

3. Using one slice of rye as the base, simply stack the cubes randomly, three cubes deep by three cubes high (total: 27 cubes).

4. Make sure you don't stack the same meat or cheese cube beside each other. This would kill the effect.

5. Top the Cubewich with the second slice of rye.

Instruments:

Cutting board, chef's knife, toaster, real Rubik's Cube (as prop and template)

   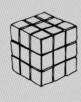

Step 2

* *Quirky Cube Facts*

- Erno Rubik invented the real Rubik's Cube in 1974 to help explain 3-D geometry.

- Worldwide sales of Rubik's Cubes exceed 300 million.

- Ailments associated with excessive "cubing" include "cubaholism" and "Rubik's wrist".

- The Cube has even inspired an art movement called Rubikubism.

- The largest Cube in the world is 9.8 feet (3 meters) tall and weighs 1,102 pounds (500 kg).

- The fastest recorded time to solve the Cube in competition is 7.08 seconds.

Great for
● Kids!

The Pac-Manwich

And while we're talkin' 80s, how could I not create an insanewich that looks like PAC-MAN? But this is no ordinary PAC-MAN. Oh no, this one gets its name by using actual Manwich mix as its filling. You remember Manwich—that sloppy joe sandwich sauce that's been around for decades? It's now being reinvented in PAC-MAN form!

You'll Need:

- **4** ounces ground beef
- **8** ounces of Manwich® sauce
- **1** slice of cornbread
- **4** raisins

Instruments:

Nonstick skillet, 2½-inch diameter round cookie cutter, chef's knife

Assembly:

1. Brown the ground beef in skillet over medium heat for 5–7 minutes. Drain.

2. Add Manwich mix and cook for 7 minutes until liquid is reduced, stirring occasionally.

3. Pile the mixture onto one side of a plate.

4. Using the cookie cutter, cut a circle out of the cornbread, then cut a pie-shaped wedge out of the circle using your knife. That'll be the mouth.

5. Place the cornbread on top of the Manwich and use one raisin for the eye.

6. Line up the rest of the raisins so that Pac-Manwich is in line to eat them.

OM NOM NOM NOM NOM

The Squeeze Playwich

A chapter about games surely needs an insanewich dedicated to America's favorite pastime. This grand slam of a sammy's got genuine ballpark franks between sourdough pretzels. It's sure to be a hit with sluggers, base stealers, and stadium fans alike.

You'll Need:

- **3** hot dogs
- **2** fresh sourdough pretzels (large)
  yellow mustard
- **½** cup peanuts

Assembly:

1. Boil or grill the doggies for 5–7 minutes.
2. Place them on one pretzel and squirt with yellow mustard in a zigzag pattern for presentation. Top with the second pretzel.
3. Serve with peanuts.

Stadium Dogs

If you're actually fortunate enough to be at the World Series, don't pass up baseball's ultimate sandwich: the stadium dog!

In *The Ultimate Baseball Road-Trip: A Fan's Guide to Major League Stadiums*, Josh Pahigian and Kevin O'Connell reveal where to find the ten best stadium dogs:

1. *Miller's Dog*
   McAfee Coliseum, Oakland

2. *The Fenway Frank*
   Fenway Park, Boston

3. *Nathan's Hot Dog*
   Yankee Stadium, New York

4. *Hebrew National Dog*
   Safeco Field, Seattle

5. *Met Jumbo Dog*
   The Metrodome, Minneapolis

6. *Aaron's Hot Dog*
   Shea Stadium, New York

7. *The Hunter's Dog*
   New Busch Stadium, St. Louis

8. *Grilled Blue Jay Dog*
   Rogers Center, Toronto

9. *Schweigert Hot Dog*
   Kauffman Stadium, Kansas City

10. *Hot Dog Heaven, The Bison Dog*
    Turner Field, Atlanta

Reel in your hunger!

The Granoagie PBJCC

Anglers often take snacks if they'll be on the water all day. But with little protein, a granola bar alone just ain't gonna cut it. This granola hoagie adds peanut butter and cream cheese for increased protein so anglers can stay out longer and increase their chances of landing that lunker.

You'll Need:

1 granola bar of your choice

2 tablespoons peanut butter

2 tablespoons strawberry jam

2 tablespoons cream cheese

Assembly:

1. With the chef's knife, carefully cut the granola bar in half lengthwise.

2. Separate into two slices of "bread."

3. Spread a layer each of peanut butter, jam, and cream cheese on one slice of granola bread and top with the other.

Instruments:

Chef's knife, chopping board

 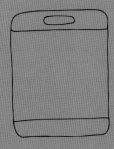

Tic Tac Tofurky!

Carrot O's may have won the first game. But the person who wins eleven gets crowned
Tic Tac Tofurky champ! And look what the prize is: a Tofurky sandwich loaded with
veggie goodness. So concentrate!

You'll Need:

- **2** slices white bread
- **1** tablespoon store-bought red pepper spread
- **3** slices Tofurky
- **1** leaf frisée lettuce
- **1** cucumber
- **½** red bell pepper
- **½** medium-sized carrot
- **1** fresh chive strand

Instruments:

Bread knife, vegetable peeler, chef's knife, ruler,
kitchen shears

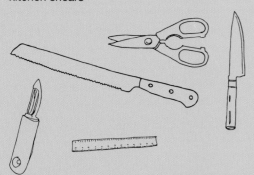

Assembly:

1. Stack two slices of bread and cut the crusts off with bread knife to form two square slices. Smear red pepper spread on one slice of bread, then stack three slices of Tofurky on top of the spread, folding each in half. Place the frisee on top of the Tofurky and top the sandwich with the second slice of bread.

2. Using a vegetable peeler, peel one long strip of skin from the cucumber. From that peel, cut four ¼-inch thick strips using the chef's knife and ruler.

3. Follow the directions for Skinning Peppers Alive in The Unique Techniques section on page 19.

4. From one segment of the skinned bell pepper, cut two long, ¼-inch slivers.

5. Place two of the cucumber strips parallel to each other and vertically on top of the sandwich. They should each be about two inches from the left and right edge of the sandwich. Cut any excess cucumber strip hanging over the edge of the sandwich with kitchen shears.

6. Place the two remaining cucumber strips parallel to each other and horizontally on top of the sandwich. They should each be about 2 inches from the top and bottom edge of the sandwich. Cut any cucumber strip that's hanging over the edge of the sandwich with kitchen shears.

7. Cut the pepper slivers into six 1-inch pieces and place two slivers in an "X" formation on the top left square, two slivers in an "X" formation in the right middle square, and two slivers in an "X" formation in the bottom-right square.

8. Cut three cross sections from the middle of the carrot and place them diagonally.

9. Place the chive striking through the three winning carrot O's.

A sandwich for when you're bored and hungry!

Step 2

Step 4

Makes two dice
hors d'oeuvres

Sandwich Dice Hors D'oeuvres

If you've been rolling dice at the casino for hours, it might be time to step away from the table and realize that these Vegas-style sammies are your only sure bet. Yep, it's about time to lay off the craps and have a bite.

You'll Need:

- **2** large carrots
- **1** small sandwich wrap
- **2** tablespoons sour cream
- squeeze of lemon
- **1** tablespoon fresh chives, chopped

Instruments:

Chef's knife, ruler, green edible marker, toothpick, bowl

Assembly:

1. Using a chef's knife, cut a 1-inch cube from each of the two large carrots. Cut them from the stem end where the carrots are thickest.

2. Using the ruler and chef's knife, cut four 1-inch squares from the sandwich wrap. Place each carrot cube on top of one wrap square and top the cubes with the remaining two squares.

3. Draw the dots on all sides with the marker, making sure the single dot is on top.

4. Insert toothpick into the single dot of one die.

5. For the dip: In a bowl, mix sour cream with squeeze of lemon and chives.

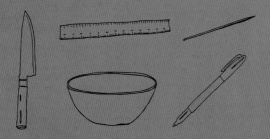

Quit the craps and give these dicey morsels a shot.

ch. **3**

067

The Playful Palette Sandwich

Hey, who's the sandwich artist here? Perhaps some bohemian who passes the days dabbling in psychedelic oils. Or Warhol himself? I dunno, but whoever it is, that person clearly has a good palate.

You'll Need:

2 slices white bread

8 ounces egg whites (from carton)

10–15 drops each of red, green, blue, and yellow food coloring

4 teaspoons canola oil

½ small avocado, diced

2 ounces canned corn niblets, drained

½ tablespoon olive oil

squeeze of lemon

2 tablespoons fresh cilantro, chopped

Instruments:

Apple corer, 4 cups, nonstick skillet, 4 spoons, spatula, bowl

Assembly:

1. Using the template provided with this recipe and the bread-carving technique described on page 17, cut out the shape required for this sandwich (palette).

2. Using the apple corer, stamp a hole out of one slice of bread, right beside the thumb indent portion of the palette.

3. Evenly divide 8 ounces of egg whites into four separate cups (about 2 ounces per cup). In one cup, add red food color, in the second cup, add green color, in the third, blue, and in the fourth, yellow. Mix each with a clean spoon.

4. Add a teaspoon of canola oil to a nonstick skillet over medium-low heat. Add the red egg mix to the pan, cook for 3 minutes, flip with spatula, and cook for another 2 minutes. Remove colored omelet from heat and set aside.

5. Repeat step 4 using the remaining colored egg mixes.

6. Using the apple corer, stamp a round from the center of each colored omelet.

7. In a bowl, add avocado, corn, olive oil, lemon, and cilantro. Mix thoroughly and spoon over top of the bread slice that you didn't stamp the hole into. Top the sandwich with the hole-punched bread.

8. Arrange the red egg circle at the top of the palette, then the green, blue, and yellow, following along the side.

TEMPLATE

Eat your sandwich in full color.

The Salmon Salad Dartboardwich

If a pub game like darts is officially recognized as a sport, why can't sandwich eating qualify as well? After all, the two activities have one very important thing in common: you can enjoy a beer while doing both. Let's start the rally, shall we?

You'll Need:

- **4** slices dark rye bread
- **½** orange bell pepper
- **¼** red bell pepper
- **1** 3½-inch diameter round slice of provolone
- **3** ounces Atlantic salmon (from can)
- **1½** tablespoons mayo
- **1** tablespoon fresh chives, chopped
- **2** squeezes of lemon
- **1** baby carrot

Instruments:

Bread knife, 5-inch diameter round cookie cutter, 2½-inch diameter round cookie cutter, 2-inch diamter round cookie cutter, apple corer, bowl, 1 real dart flight (the non-pointy end of the dart), 1 toothpick

Assembly:

1. Stack the bread slices. Simultaneously slice the bottom crusts from all four slices.

2. Take two of those slices and lay them flat beside each other so the cut ends are butting up against each other. This will allow you to make a much larger "dart board."

3. With the 5-inch diameter round cookie cutter, stamp out a circle from the two slices of bread that are beside each other. This will form one circle from the two slices.

4. Repeat steps 2 and 3 with the remaining two slices of bread.

5. Follow the directions for Skinning Peppers Alive in The Unique Techniques section on page 19 for the orange bell pepper.

6. Using the 2-inch diameter round cookie cutter, stamp out a circle from the orange bell pepper.

7. Follow the directions for Skinning Peppers Alive in The Unique Techniques section on page 19 for the red bell pepper.

8. Using the apple corer, stamp out the bull's-eye from the red bell pepper.

9. Using the 2½-inch diameter round cookie cutter, stamp out a centered inner circle from the round slice of provolone cheese. You will be left with a ring.

10. In a bowl combine the salmon, mayo, chives, and lemon.

11. Place the first two slices of bread that were cut into one circle on a plate beside each other so the flat ends are butting up against each other. Spread the salmon salad on top.

continued ➤➤

12. Top the sandwich with the second two slices of bread that were cut into a circle.

13. Place the provolone circle on top of the sandwich. Make sure it's centered.

14. Place the orange bell pepper round within the provolone circle and the red bell pepper round as the bull's-eye.

15. Poke the toothpick into one end of the baby carrot.

16. Cut a small slice into the other end of the baby carrot with the chef's knife, making sure not to cut all the way through the carrot.

17. Turn the carrot one quarter and make another slice to form an "X." Slide the dart flight into this X.

18. Poke the baby carrot dart into the sandwich's bull's-eye.

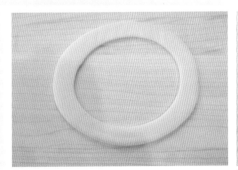

Step 9

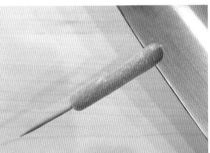

Step 16

tough guywiches

So ya think yer a tough guy, huh? But are you tough enough to brave these bruisers? Get ready dude, 'cuz Tough Guywiches have officially joined the mix. They're rough. They're mean. They're packin' some punch! Get rid of the loofahs, facial scrubs, and duvet covers 'cuz this grouping will really separate the men from the boys.

The Jersey Shore Lunch

This guido torpedo sports four big Italian meatballs hanging out on a sub bun and talkin' some serious cheese. They're studded with garlic (which becomes aromatic during cooking) and they're sitting on tangy tomato sauce. Luckily for them, none of the sauce has messed up their pristine toothpick faux-hawk hairdos.

You'll Need:

12 ounces ground beef

4 ounces bread crumbs

1 egg

salt and pepper to taste

2 tablespoons olive oil

4 slices mozzarella cheese

8 cloves garlic, whole

1 Italian sub bun

4–5 ounces of your favorite tomato sauce

8 diced squares of red bell pepper

Instruments:

Bowl, baking sheet, chef's knife, 20-25 toothpicks (assorted red, white, and green)

Assembly:

1. Preheat oven to 400°F.

2. Place ground beef in bowl and add bread crumbs, egg, salt, and pepper. With clean hands, combine thoroughly.

3. Divide mixture into four equal parts and use your hands to roll each into a large meatball.

4. Pour olive oil onto baking sheet and spread so it covers the sheet.

5. Place meatballs on baking sheet and cook in oven for 30–35 minutes until cooked all the way through. Remove from oven and allow to cool to room temperature.

6. When cooled, cut each meatball in half. Place one piece of cheese on top of the bottom half of each meatball then top with the other meatball halves.

7. Make two slits on the top half of each meatball where the eyes will be and stuff one clove of garlic into each eye slit.

8. Place meatballs back in the oven for about 4 minutes or until the cheese melts. Remove the meatballs from the oven.

9. Slice bun almost completely in half lengthwise. Pour tomato sauce on the bottom half of the bun.

10. Place four meatballs on the bun (Don't worry if all don't fit.) Pour drippings from pan over the meatballs.

11. Add diced red bell pepper pupils to the garlic eyeballs.

12. Arrange red, white and green toothpicks on the crowns of the four meatballs to form faux-hawks.

13. Remove toothpicks before eating.

Before going out, always remember to sandwich and shave.

The Spaghetti and Greaseball

Gotta get ready to go out and there's no time to cook? Hey, chillax, paisano! All ya gotta do is bust out a can of spaghetti and meatballs, give it a quick nuke, and make this sandwich in no time. Fuggedaboutit! It's got Italian bread with parmesan cheese fried right into the crust. And to save even more time, just eat and shave at once. Then badda bing! You're done!

You'll Need:

- **2** slices of Italian bread
- **1** clove garlic
- **2** ounces parmesan cheese
- **1** can store-bought spaghetti and meatballs

Instruments:

Nonstick skillet, cheese grater, toaster, bowl

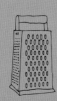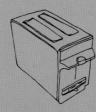

Assembly:

1. Rub two slices of Italian bread with clove of garlic (all sides).
2. Heat nonstick skillet over medium-low heat.
3. Grate parmesan cheese right into skillet and allow to melt.
4. Place one slice of bread in skillet for 2–3 minutes until cheese sticks to bread.
5. Remove skillet from heat and set cheesy bread aside.
6. Toast second slice of bread in toaster. Set aside.
7. Open can of spaghetti and meatballs and empty into a bowl.
8. Microwave at medium heat for 3–5 minutes, or according to directions.
9. Place non-cheesy bread on plate and flop spaghetti and meatballs on top.
10. Place cheesy slice on top of pasta, cheese side facing up.

The Fight Club

In the world of yummy, back-alley sandwich brawls, The Fight Club sandwich is known as the scrappiest. What makes it so tasty? Crisp Boston lettuce, avocado, chicken breast, bacon…and a punishing right hook powered by savory naan bread.

You'll Need:

- **4** ounces cooked chicken breast, sliced
  salt and pepper to taste
- **4** slices of bacon
- **2** pieces onion naan (or pita bread)
- **2** leaves of Boston lettuce
- **1** slice marble cheddar
- **2** slices of tomato
- **½** avocado, sliced
- **1** tablespoon mayo

Instruments:

Chef's knife, nonstick skillet, black edible marker

Assembly:

1. Preheat oven to 375°F.

2. Season chicken breast with salt and pepper and bake for 15–20 minutes. Slice thinly and set aside.

3. Fry slices of bacon until crisp or microwave precooked, store-bought bacon for 60–90 seconds.

4. Using the template provided with this recipe, and the bread-carving technique described on page 17, cut out the bread shape required for this sandwich (fist).

5. On top of one piece, add as much detail, (finger separation, knuckles, outlining, etc) as you wish using black edible marker.

6. On top of the other piece, stack the lettuce, cheese, tomato, avocado, bacon, and sliced chicken breast, then slather with mayo.

7. Top the sandwich with the first piece, making sure the fist details face upwards.

THE RULES OF THE FIGHT CLUB SANDWICH

The Rules of Fight Club apply both to groups of underground brawlers and deliciously scrappy sandwiches:

#1 - The first rule of The Fight Club Sandwich is you do not talk about eating The Fight Club Sandwich.

#2 - The second rule of The Fight Club Sandwich is you DO NOT talk about eating The Fight Club Sandwich.

#3 - If a sandwich gets devoured, lettuce goes limp, fillings fall out, then the sandwich is toast.

#4 - Only two slices can be used for every one sandwich.

#5 - Stack only one slice at a time.

#6 - No plates, no cutlery.

#7 - Ingredients will be piled on only as high as they have to be.

#8 - If this is your first time eating The Fight Club Sandwich, you have to finish it.

TEMPLATE

The Cold Cut Cage Match

The next time you grab those little round mini-cheeses covered in red wax, hang on to the netting they come in. It looks like chain link fence and can be used to construct this octagon-shaped insanewich. You and your pals will enjoy this one the next time you gather to watch mixed martial artists duke it out on pay-per-view.

You'll Need:

- **2** large pieces of flatbread
- **2** tablespoons grainy Dijon mustard
- **2** ounces radicchio
- **2** ounces arugula
- **5** slices Genoa salami
- **2** slices rosemary-infused ham
- **3** slices smoked chicken breast (deli meat)

Instruments:

Kitchen shears, 1 bag of netting from mini-cheeses (Mini Babybel® Original), 8 toothpicks, 2 small toy fighters (about 2 inches tall)

Assembly:

TO PREP CAGE

1. Using kitchen shears, cut the metal fastener from the top and bottom of the mini-cheese netting. This leaves you with a netting "tube" to work with.

2. From this tube, cut three lengths that are approximately 2 inches wide by 6 inches long.

3. Thread four toothpicks through the first length and four through the second.

4. From the third length, cut two smaller 2-inch lengths.

5. Set all netting aside.

FOR THE SANDWICH

1. Using the template provided for this recipe and the bread-carving technique described on page 17, cut out the shape required for this sandwich (octagon).

2. Smear the grainy Dijon on one piece of bread.

3. On top of the mustard, layer the radicchio, arugula, Genoa salami, rosemary-infused ham, smoked chicken breast, and top with second piece.

4. Carefully insert toothpick-threaded cages into top of sandwich. Make sure each toothpick lines up with a corresponding corner of the octagon. Do not insert toothpicks too close to the edge.

5. There will be a gap in the cage on two opposing sides. Fill these in with the extra 2-inch lengths you cut earlier.

6. Place the fighters in the ring.

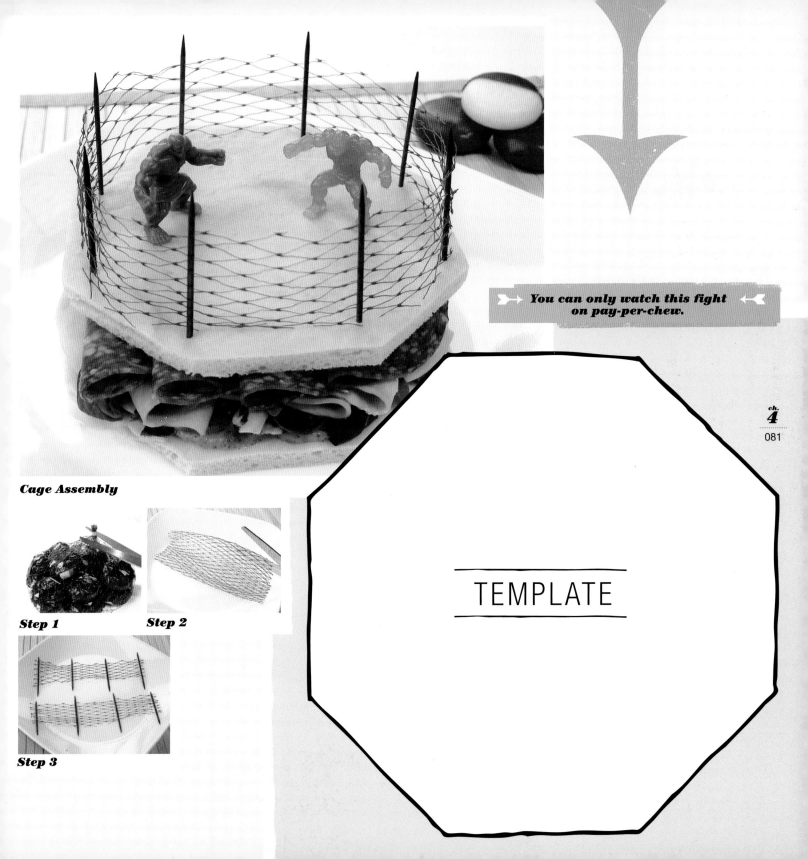

You can only watch this fight on pay-per-chew.

Cage Assembly

Step 1

Step 2

Step 3

TEMPLATE

The Hulk Hoagie

Hulk Hogan famously said: "Say your prayers and eat your vitamins!" But I say, if you want 24-inch pythons just like the Hulkster, all you gotta do is eat one of these Hulk Hoagies each day. Here's what I used to make it: String cheese forms the brows, handlebar 'stache, and skullet hair; a red pepper makes up the bandanna; and a crusty submarine bun was used to mimic heavily suntanned skin. Please note: a regular napkin should never be served with The Hulk Hoagie. You gotta use a real red bandanna to honor balding tough guys everywhere.

You'll Need:

- **1** 9-inch submarine bun
- **2** tablespoons yellow mustard
- **1** large leaf Romaine lettuce
- **2** slices jalapeño Havarti cheese
- **4** slices oven-roasted chicken breast (deli meat)
- **3** slices salami
- **1** small Kirby cucumber
- **1** large pimento olive
- **1** large red bell pepper
- **4** cylinders of string cheese
- **1** small cherry tomato

Instruments:

Bread knife, steak knife, chef's knife

Step 7

Assembly:

1. Using the bread knife, slice the submarine bun in half lengthwise to create a top and bottom.
2. On the bottom half, squeeze yellow mustard and then layer Romaine lettuce, jalapeño Havarti slices, oven-roasted chicken breast, and salami.
3. Top the sandwich with the second bun half.
4. Using a steak knife, carve a small wedge out of the top half of the sandwich to create the mouth.
5. For the eyes, slice two cross sections from the cucumber approximately ½-inch thick and two cross sections from the pimento olive of the same thickness.
6. Place the olive rounds on top of the cucumber rounds. The natural moisture will keep them sticking together. Set aside.
7. For the red pepper bandanna: cut the top off a red bell pepper, then hollow out the bottom part of the pepper using your steak knife.
8. For the handlebar 'stache: separate both ends of one cylinder of string cheese into as many "hairs" as you can. Just be sure to leave the middle still stuck to keep the strings together and maintain the handlebar effect.
9. For the hair: Separate another cylinder of string cheese almost to the end, making as many "hairs" as you can. Just be sure to leave about ½-inch at the end still stuck to keep the strings together.
10. Repeat step 9 for the hair on the other side of Hoagie's head.
11. For the eyebrows: cut a 1½-inch length from the last cylinder of string cheese and separate that length in half and then one of those halves in quarters.
12. Separate and frill out the ends from each quarter piece.
13. Lay the hair down on your plate or serving platter, spreading out the flowing locks.
14. Fit the red pepper bandanna on the Hoagie's head and place the whole sandwich on top of the cheese strings to make it look like the "hair" is peeking out from behind the bandanna.
15. Place the eyebrows below the bandanna, the eyes below the eyebrows, the cherry tomato nose centered below the two eyes, and the handlebar 'stache below the nose.

This recipe makes one wrap (use additional wrap flavors for other three)

The Mean Sardine

Imagine tearing into a can of sardines and these four fishy wraps pop out! What a tasty surprise that'd be. After all, it's tough to beat savory sardine wraps slathered with lemon aioli. Plus, each one is totally a one-hander, so you can eat and channel surf at once.

You'll Need:

½	teaspoon garlic, chopped (fresh or store-bought)
1	tablespoon mayo
	squeeze of lemon
	sandwich wrap (use your favorite flavor)
2	ounces fennel, sliced thinly
2	leaves of lettuce
3–4	sardines from can

Assembly:

1. Prepare the aioli by combining garlic, mayo, and lemon in a bowl. Mix thoroughly.

2. Lay your favorite flavor wrap flat and smear half with aioli; avoid spreading it too close to the edges.

3. Lay the sliced fennel down on top of the aioli and then place the lettuce leaves over the fennel.

4. Remove three or four sardines from a freshly opened can and lay them on top of the lettuce.

5. Roll the wrap as tightly as possible and cut out a 4-inch segment from the middle to showcase the ingredients.

NOTE: *Repeat steps 1–5 with 3 additional wrap flavors*

Instruments:

Bowl, chef's knife, chopping board

➤ *Packed like sardines in a tin!*

The Last Samuwich

If yer thinkin' it's a sushi night, try this sandwich, which was inspired by the Samurai (the ultimate Japanese tough guy). It's got sashimi-grade salmon and tuna, which means no need to turn on the oven tonight. And you can eat it with disposable chopsticks for less clean up. Looks like you just freed up a bit of time this evening.

You'll Need:

1 tablespoon mayonnaise

½ teaspoon prepared wasabi horseradish

3 plain rice crackers

2 ounces sashimi-grade salmon

6 whole fresh cilantro leaves

2 ounces sashimi-grade tuna

2 ounces wasabi peas

Instruments:

Bowl

Assembly:

1. In a bowl, combine mayo and wasabi. Mix thoroughly.

2. Place first rice cracker on plate and dollop with half of mayo mixture.

3. Layer salmon on top of mayo and place half of the cilantro leaves over the salmon.

4. Layer the second cracker next and dollop with remaining mayo mixture.

5. Layer tuna, remaining cilantro, and third cracker.

6. Serve with wasabi peas.

➤ *An honorable warrior 'wich.*

Deviled Egg Drillwich

Without a doubt, power tools bring out the man's man in almost any guy. Admittedly though, you're not gonna reno the basement with this scrumptious sammy strapped to your toolbelt. After all, it's powered by egg salad and has an asparagus drill bit!

You'll Need:

- **2** hardboiled eggs, peeled and chopped fine
- **3** teaspoons mayo
- **¼** teaspoon smoked paprika
- **2** tablespoons fresh dill, chopped

  Salt and pepper to taste
- **2** pieces of pita bread
- **1** small zucchini
- **1** small asparagus

Instruments:

Bowl, chef's knife, 1 large skewer, spoon, vegetable peeler, chopping board

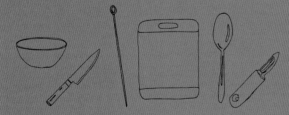

Assembly:

1. In a bowl, combine eggs, mayo, smoked paprika, dill, salt, and pepper. Mix thoroughly and set aside.

2. Using the template provided in this recipe and the bread-carving technique described on page 17, cut out the shape required for this sandwich (drill body).

3. Using the chef's knife, cut a 3-inch length (including stem) from the tip of the zucchini. Reserve the rest of the zucchini.

4. Using the skewer, poke a hole straight through the center of the zucchini.

5. Cut the tip off the asparagus approximately 3 inches from the top and slide the cut end into the hole in the zucchini.

6. Spoon the egg salad onto one of the drill body bread pieces and top the sandwich with the other.

7. Using a vegetable peeler, peel off a layer of skin from the reserved zucchini. On a chopping board, cut out a small rectangle from the skin about ½ inch wide by 2 inches long.

8. Place the skin on top of the drill body to mimic the brand label.

9. Place the zucchini-asparagus combo up against the front of the drill body.

Do you keep this in your toolbox or lunchbox?

TEMPLATE

Step 4

Beer Dunkwiches

Say hello to the Oreos 'n' milk of the tough guy world. That's right brother, next time you're about to kick back in front of the tube to watch a Dirty Harry flick, skip the cookies and skim and dunk a few of these sammies in your brewski!

You'll Need:

1	stick of butter
2	ounces of chives, finely chopped
10	small slices of light party rye bread
3	slices of Muenster cheese
2	slices of Edam cheese
1	pint of your favorite beer

Instruments:

2½-inch diameter round cookie cutter, resealable container

Assembly:

1. For the compound butter: In a resealable container, thoroughly incorporate room-temperature butter and chives. Place mixture in refrigerator for 5 minutes to stiffen slightly.

2. Stack ten slices of party rye bread in pairs for a total of five stacks.

3. Using the round cookie cutter, stamp out a round from each two-slice stack. Separate each stack to produce ten uniform round slices.

4. Using the same cookie cutter, stamp out three rounds from the Muenster and two rounds from the Edam.

5. Remove the compound butter from the refrigerator and spread onto five of the round slices. Each slice will require about ½ a teaspoon of compound butter.

6. Place one round of cheese onto each buttered slice and top each little sandwich with one of the five remaining unbuttered slices of bread.

7. Using a knife, cut a 1-inch radius into one of the sandwiches and slide it onto the lip of a pint glass like you would an orange slice.

8. Top the pint with your favorite beer, stack the remaining sandwiches.

The sandwiches you dunk in beer!

One Tough Cookie

If this sandwich could talk smack, it'd say: "That's the way the cookie crumbles, sucka!" And you thought tough guys couldn't possibly enjoy sweet treats. Well, they can, and in case you're wondering why this 'wich isn't in the dessert chapter, it's 'cuz it's far too tough for those sweetie pies.

You'll Need:

2 chocolate chocolate chip cookies (or cookies of your choice)

White frosting

Red frosting

1 scoop vanilla ice cream

Instruments:

2 action figure arms

Assembly:

1. Rip the arms off your favorite tough-guy action figure. Set aside.

2. With white frosting, draw two dots for eyes, mad-looking eyebrows, and a zig-zag mouth on one cookie. Freeze that cookie for at least 10 minutes.

3. Remove cookie from freezer and dab a red frosting pupil on top of each white frosting eye.

4. Spread one scoop of vanilla ice cream onto the second cookie and top with first cookie (make sure the face is facing upward).

5. Jab the arms into the ice cream on either side of the sandwich.

6. Freeze the whole cookie sandwich for at least another hour so the arms become solidly lodged.

7. Serve directly from freezer. Remove appendages before eating.

Let's get ready to crumble!...
I mean rumble!

'wichy
woman

51

5

Lunch still up in the air? Lookin' for the perfect fun family snack? Or just wanna spice up your next get-together? Take notice, 'cuz you're about to hit the mother lode of insanewiches! Kick your garden variety salads and routine wraps to the curb and feast your eyes on these 'wichy creations.

Bridgewiches

You're hosting the next bridge night and you want to serve something different. Whip up some of these bite-size tea sandwiches and you're bound to impress the group. And when your friend hosts bridge night next week, she's sure to follow suit...

You'll Need:

- **2** slices white bread
- **2** slices dark rye bread
- **2** slices raisin bread
- **2** slices whole wheat bread
- **1** heaping tablespoon orange marmalade
- **1** heaping tablespoon cream cheese
- **1** heaping tablespoon strawberry jam
- **1** heaping tablespoon smooth peanut butter

Instruments:

Chopping Board, 4 tablespoons, heart-shaped cookie cutter, club-shaped cookie cutter, diamond-shaped cookie cutter, spade-shaped cookie cutter (all approximately 3½ inches tall by 3¼ inches wide)

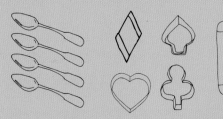

Assembly:

1. Lay one slice each of white, dark rye, raisin, and whole wheat bread beside each other on top of a chopping board.

2. Spread the orange marmalade on the white bread and top this sandwich with the other slice of white bread.

3. Spread the cream cheese on the dark rye bread and top this sandwich with the other slice of dark rye bread.

4. Spread the strawberry jam on the raisin bread and top this sandwich with the other slice of raisin bread.

5. Spread the peanut butter on the whole wheat bread and top this sandwich with the other slice of whole wheat bread.

6. Using the heart-shaped cookie cutter, stamp a heart shape from the white bread sandwich.

7. Using the club-shaped cookie cutter, stamp a club shape from the dark rye bread sandwich.

8. Using the diamond-shaped cookie cutter, stamp a diamond shape from the raisin bread sandwich.

9. Using the spade-shaped cookie cutter, stamp a spade shape from the whole wheat bread sandwich.

10. Place each suit sandwich on the same plate.

* RAISE THE MARTINI BAR

Nothing goes better with your cosmo 'wich than a martini. Here are three tasty variations:

I'll have my martini sandwich stacked. Not stirred.

COSMOPOLITAN

- **2** ounces vodka (chilled)
- **1** ounce orange liqueur
- **1** ounce cranberry juice
- **1** ounce freshly squeezed lime juice
- **4** ice cubes

LYCHEE MARTINI

- **2** ounces vodka (chilled)
- **1** ounce lychee liqueur
- **1** dash lychee juice (or lychee syrup)
- **1** lychee, peeled and pitted
- **1** maraschino cherry
- **4** ice cubes

CHOCOLATE MARTINI

- **2** ounces vodka (chilled)
- **1** ounce chocolate liqueur
- **½** ounce dark crème de cacao
- **4** ice cubes

Instructions for each martini:

Shake all ingredients vigorously in a cocktail shaker and strain into a chilled martini glass.

Cosmo Martiniwich

For this one, I used ingredients that mIrror the flavors of a Cosmo. Cranberry juice is replaced with a cranberry muffin. Orange liqueur is swapped with orange cruller and real orange segments. The result is a cocktail look-alike that you can't order when you're at the bar with friends.

You'll Need:

- **1** orange
- **1** cosmopolitan martini (recipe on previous page)
- **1** cranberry muffin (top only)
- **½** orange cruller
- **1** cranberry
- **1** slice of lime

Instruments:

Chef's knife, food processor, martini glass, strainer, toothpick, plastic container

Assembly:

1. Peel and segment orange using your chef's knife. Place in a plastic container.

2. Make cosmopolitan martini following the directions on previous page.

3. Pour the martini over the orange slices, cover the container, and let them soak for one hour in the fridge.

4. While the oranges are soaking, remove the top from one cranberry muffin and pulse in food processor until fine. Place mixture in the bottom of the martini glass as the bottom "slice."

5. Remove oranges from fridge and strain. Layer oranges on top of cranberry muffin mixture.

6. Place cruller in food processor and pulse until fine.

7. Place cruller mixture on top of oranges to create the top "slice." The crumbs should be centered in the glass so that you can still see the oranges.

8. Pierce cranberry with toothpick and place it into the top of your sandwich.

9. Cut halfway into the slice of lime and place on the rim of glass.

Flip-Phone Cellwich

The good thing about *this* phone is you'll never need to go digging through your purse to find it. And it looks so realistic you'll wanna use it to text your best friend: "omg, gonna eat yummiest sammich EVAR!!! u gotta try. ttyl." What makes it so delish? It's got a pastrami call display and Swiss cheese keypad, so when hunger calls, it's easy to answer.

You'll Need:

1 slice white bread

2 slices dark rye

3 slices pastrami

2 slices Swiss cheese

Instruments:

Kitchen shears, toothpick, chef's knife, ruler

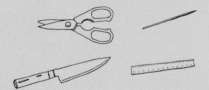

Assembly:

1. Using the templates provided for this recipe and the bread-carving technique described on page 17, cut out the bread shapes required for this sandwich (one top portion of phone from the white slice, and two slices of dark rye as the phone middle and bottom). Set aside.

2. On the bottom phone base slice, place two slices of the pastrami and one slice of Swiss cheese.

3. Using the technique for cutting deli meat with shears on page 19, remove the excess pastrami and cheese.

4. Place the second slice of dark rye on top of the pastrami and cheese. Now the "tongue" on the white bread will fit into the "groove" on the dark rye bread.

5. Use the toothpick to prop up the white bread from behind so it suspends at approximately a 45° angle. One point of the toothpick will be on the plate and the other end will be holding the bread slice up.

6. From the second slice of Swiss cheese, cut nine squares each about ½ by ½ inch in size, using your chef's knife. Cut an additional rectangle about ¾ by 2 inches in size.

7. Place the nine squares of cheese on the top slice of dark rye in three rows of three and place the rectangular piece of cheese right above the squares.

8. From the remaining slice of pastrami, cut one rectangle about 2 inches by 2½ inches and another about ½ by 1½ inches, using your chef's knife.

9. Place the larger rectangle on top of the white slice of bread and the smaller one on top of the Swiss cheese rectangle.

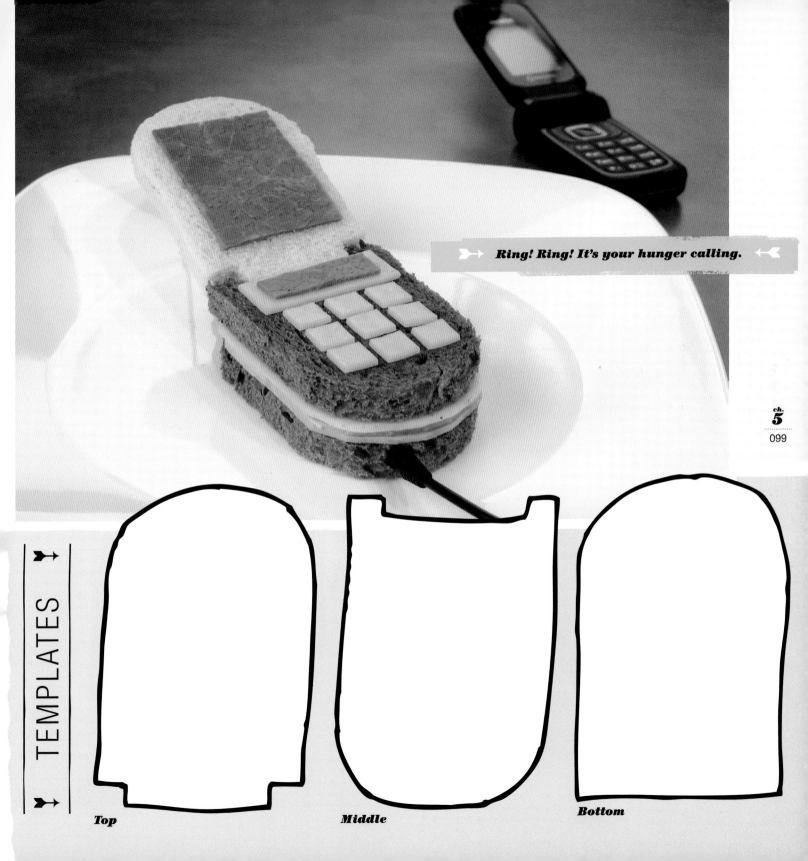

Ring! Ring! It's your hunger calling.

TEMPLATES

Top

Middle

Bottom

TEMPLATE

A sandwich grilled to perfection!

The Steak 'N' Potatwich

Step 2

Who said steak and potatoes can't be sandwichified? This meaty-potatoey dish turns the classic combo on its head with sweet potato as the "bread." Can you say al fresco dining? With grill marks like that, this 'wich was meant to be eaten outdoors!

You'll Need:

- **1** large sweet potato
- **1** medium yellow onion
- **1** small eggplant
- **3** tablespoons olive oil
  salt and pepper to taste
- **1** ¾-inch medallion of filet mignon (ask your butcher or meat counter to cut it to this thickness)
- **1** tablespoon honey mustard

Instruments:

Grill pan, chef's knife, chopping board, tongs, toothpick

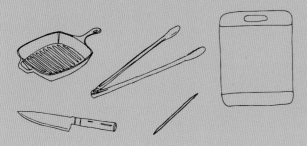

Assembly:

1. Preheat grill pan on stovetop over medium heat.
2. Cut two ½-inch cross-sections from the sweet potato.
3. With the template provided for this recipe and the technique described on page 17, cut out the shapes required for this sandwich (sweet potato bread slice shapes).
4. Next, cut a ½-inch round out of the yellow onion and cut a ½-inch section out of the eggplant on the bias.
5. Brush both sides of all veggies (including sweet potato) with olive oil and season with salt.
6. Place the slices of sweet potato bread on the grill and cook each side for 5–6 minutes or until nicely charred. Set aside.
7. Brush both sides of the filet with olive oil and season with salt and pepper. Grill each side for 4 minutes. Remove from grill and let rest.
8. While meat is resting, grill onion and eggplant on both sides for 2–3 minutes or until nicely charred.
9. To assemble, lay one sweet potato slice on a plate and stack the onion, eggplant, and filet on top. Dollop the honey mustard on the filet and top with the second sweet potato slice.
10. Poke toothpick into top.

The Wildflower 'Wich

The gardener who grew this open-faced specimen must've planted some pretty special seeds: what type of flower has basil petals, egg white pollen, and an asparagus stem? If you're itching to use your green thumb, break out the gardening gloves and germinate this 'wich.

You'll Need

- **1** small plum tomato
- **1** jalapeño pepper
- **1** teaspoon olive oil
- **4** ounces liquid egg white (from container)
- **1** slice ancient grain bread (or whole wheat bread)
- **1** asparagus stalk
- **8** medium-sized basil leaves

Instruments:

Chef's knife, nonstick skillet, 3½-inch diameter round cookie cutter, spatula, toaster, chopping board

Assembly:

1. Dice tomato very finely. Set aside.

2. Slice one ½-inch thick cross-section round from the middle of a jalapeño pepper. Scrape the insides out to make a ring.

3. Add olive oil to a nonstick skillet over medium-low heat. Add whites and scramble for about 4 minutes.

4. Toast bread and use cookie cutter to stamp out a round from the bread.

5. Microwave asparagus for 35–45 seconds and then cut the tip off.

6. Place the toasted round on a clean chopping board (I found a plate was too small) and then the scrambled whites on top.

7. Place the jalapeño ring in the center of the whites and fill it with the finely diced tomato.

8. Place the asparagus stem so it looks like it's growing out of the bottom of the circle.

9. Evenly space the basil leaves around the circle's circumference with the points of the leaves facing out and the stems underneath the toast.

It'll be in full bloom by lunch.

Say cheese! Camembert, actually.

Step 7

The Digital Camwich

Maybe you're a hungry photog with a keen eye for sandwiches. If that's true, you'll definitely wanna give this 'wich a try. Just make sure to store it in your cooler pack and not your camera case by accident.

You'll Need:

- **2** slices thin rye bread
- **3** slices Serrano ham
- **3** ounces Camembert cheese (3 slices from a wheel)
- **1** slice Gouda cheese
- **1** $\frac{1}{16}$-inch slice of cucumber
- **1** $\frac{1}{2}$-inch slice of zucchini
- **1** $\frac{5}{8}$-inch slice of carrot
- **1** $\frac{1}{4}$-inch slice of carrot
- **1** cucumber

Instruments:

Bread knife, chef's knife, apple corer, toothpick, vegetable peeler, ruler

Assembly:

1. Using a bread knife, cut two slices of bread into 4-inch by 3-inch rectangles.
2. Stack the slices of Serrano ham and using the chef's knife, cut them into a 4-inch by 3-inch rectangle.
3. On top of one slice of bread, stack the Serrano ham and Camembert cheese. Top with the second slice of bread.
4. From the slice of Gouda, cut out one rectangle that's approximately 2½ by ¾ inches and place it vertically on the left side of the camwich. Using the chef's knife, cut out a small rectangle from the slice of gouda, 1 by ½ inches in size. Place it horizontally to the top right of the camwich to make the cheese flash.
5. Using the apple corer, stamp out a round from the slice of Gouda and place it beside the top of the vertical rectangle.
6. Right below the cheese flash, stack the cucumber slice, zucchini slice, and thicker carrot slice to create the extendable lens.
7. Poke a toothpick halfway into the thinner carrot slice. Break off other half of toopthpick.
8. Stick the toothpick into the top left of the camwich in between the bottom slice of bread and the Serrano to create the shutter release button.
9. Using a vegetable peeler, peel a slice of skin from a cucumber. From this slice, cut a ¼-inch thin strip. Fold the strip end to end and place the ends up beside the side of the camwich to create the wrist strap.

It'll take one big ol' glass of milk to dunk this cookie sammich!

Girls' Night Inwich

Don't even think about eating your Oreos® straight outta the package. With only a few minutes of prep, you can make this elegant, chocolatey concoction, and it's up to you whether you wanna twist 'n' dunk.

You'll Need:

9 thin, wafer-style chocolate cookies

Tube of white frosting

3 raspberries

Assembly:

1. Lay one of the cookies flat.

2. Squeeze out a layer of white frosting on top of the cookie, starting in the center of the cookie and spiraling to the outer edge.

3. Top with the next cookie.

4. Repeat steps 2 and 3 six more times. Feel free to stagger each layer a bit so the frosting is more visible.

5. Squeeze out one large dollop of frosting in the center of the top cookie.

6. Break the last cookie in half and stand one of those halves up in the top dollop of frosting.

7. Serve with the raspberries.

Luxury Vacation 'Wich

A fun way to gear up for your tropical vacation is by making this all-inclusive getaway sandwich. You'll love the luxurious, sandy pound cake beaches and deluxe fruit roll-up beach towel service. It's one of the most decadent sandwich destinations on Earth, so book now!

You'll Need:

1 golden loaf cake

3 tablespoons whipped cream

½ mango, diced

4 strawberries, halved

2 fruit roll-ups (one needs to have red in it)

1 large marshmallow

Instruments:

Bread knife, steak knife, chef's knife, kitchen shears, pink umbrella

Assembly:

1. From the cake, cut two slices lengthwise from the bottom up.

2. Stack the two pieces, and using the steak knife, cut out an island shape. Make the shape about 7 inches long and 2½ inches wide. If you'd like the island to look more realistic, you may round the edges of the top slice with your steak knife.

3. Lay one slice on the plate and dollop with whipped cream.

4. Sprinkle diced mango over top of whipped cream.

5. Randomly place strawberry halves over top.

6. Top sandwich with the second cake slice.

7. To make the beach towel: Unroll one fruit roll-up and separate it from the plastic.

8. Unroll the second fruit roll-up (with red in it) and lay the plastic from the first fruit roll-up over the inside of it. Having plastic covering both sides of this fruit roll-up will make it easier to measure and cut with shears.

9. From the red part of the fruit roll-up, cut a rough rectangle about 1 inch wide by 3 inches long.

10. Remove the plastic and place the roll-up beach towel on top of the sandwich.

11. Cut the marshmallow in half and place it at the head of the beach towel like a pillow.

12. Stick the pink umbrella in the sandwich so it shades the towel.

Call 1-800-555-WICH for travel details!

super
size
wiches

6

Got a gargantuan hankering? Love to feel full? These Supersizewiches are the biggest and best button-popping and calorie-laden 'wiches you'll ever lay eyes upon. They're heart-stoppingly good and they'll keep you full for hours. Don't bother counting calories. They're off the charts!

The Quadruple Down

When KFC launched The Double Down, everyone thought it was a hoax. Two deep-fried chicken breasts as bread?!? But as it turned out, KFC actually did test-market the sandwich to great success. When I read about the high-cal creation, I asked myself: Why stop at just two chicken breasts?…or even three? And just like that, The Quadruple Down was born!

NOTE: For this photo, I used premade chicken breasts. But I've also prepared this dish using the below made-from-scratch recipe.

You'll Need:

- **1** cup fine breadcrumbs
- **1** teaspoon salt
- **½** teaspoon pepper
- **½** teaspoon cumin
- **½** teaspoon dry mustard
- **4** four-ounce chicken breasts (feel free to flatten if your chicken breasts are thick)
- **3** slices bacon
- **3** tablespoons mayonnaise
- **1** teaspoon paprika
- **¼** teaspoon chipotle chile powder
- **2** slices pepper jack cheese
- **1** slice Swiss cheese

Assembly:

1. If making the chicken from scratch, add breadcrumbs, salt, pepper, cumin, and dry mustard to Ziploc bag.

2. Place chicken breasts inside bag and shake until completely coated.

3. Preheat oven to 400°F. Place chicken breasts on baking sheet and cook in oven for 20 to 25 minutes until golden. Remove from oven and set aside to cool.

4. Fry the bacon until crisp and drain on a paper towel.

5. In a bowl, mix mayo with paprika and chipotle chile powder. Set aside.

6. Place one chicken breast on a plate, and cover with 1 tablespoon of mayo. Lay one slice of pepper jack cheese and then one slice of bacon on top.

7. Lay the next chicken breast on and cover with 1 tablespoon of mayo. Lay one slice of Swiss cheese and then one slice of bacon on top.

8. Place the third chicken breast on and cover with 1 tablespoon of mayo. Lay one slice of pepper jack cheese and then one slice of bacon on top.

9. Top the sandwich with the final chicken breast.

Instruments:

Large Ziploc bag, baking sheet, nonstick skillet, bowl

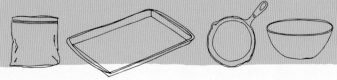

The Swine 'N' Cheese

If you're an insanewich aficionado, the best way to unwind after a long day isn't with a glass of vino at dinner. I suggest you put your feet up and enjoy a nice glass of swine 'n' cheese. 'Cuz if salted, cured meats and an assortment of cheeses in a wine glass can't get you chilled out, I dunno what will.

You'll Need:

- **5** slices rye bread, thinly sliced
- **3** slices black forest ham
- **3** slices provolone cheese
- **3** slices Genoa salami
- **3** slices yellow cheddar
- **3** slices capocollo ham, approximately 3 inches in diameter
- **3** slices mozzarella
- **3** slices pancetta
- **1** large pimento olive

NOTE: The bowl of the wine glass should be 3½ inches in diameter, while the lip needs to be 2½ inches.

Instruments:

Toaster, wine glass, round cookie cutters (1½-, 2½-, 3-, 3½-inch diameters), cutting board, 1 toothpick

Assembly:

1. Lightly toast all five slices of rye bread. Set aside.
2. Using the 1½-inch round cookie cutter, stamp out one round from one slice of toast. Place the round at the bottom of the wine glass.
3. Next, stack the three slices of black forest ham on a cutting board. Using the 2½-inch round cookie cutter, stamp out a round from the ham slices. Place in the wine glass.
4. Stack the three slices of provolone on a cutting board. Using the 3-inch round cookie cutter, stamp out a round from the provolone slices. Place in the wine glass.
5. Using the 3½-inch round cookie cutter, stamp out one round from one slice of toast. Place the round in the wine glass.
6. Stack the three slices of Genoa salami. Using the 3½-inch round cookie cutter, stamp out a round from the Genoa salami slices. Place in the wine glass.
7. Stack the three slices of cheddar. Using the 3½-inch round cookie cutter, stamp out a round from the cheddar slices. Place in the wine glass.
8. Using the 3-inch round cookie cutter, stamp out one round from one slice of toast. Place the round in the wine glass.
9. Stack the three slices of capocollo, and place in the wine glass.
10. Stack the three slices of mozzarella. Using the 3-inch round cookie cutter, stamp out a round from the mozzarella slices. Place in the wine glass.
11. Using the 3-inch round cookie cutter, stamp out one round from one slice of toast. Place the round in the wine glass.
12. Layer the pancetta slices in the wine glass. You do not need to cut them. They can be easily squeezed in.
13. Using the 2½-inch round cookie cutter, stamp out one round from the last slice of toast. Top the sandwich with this slice.
14. Pierce the olive with the toothpick and poke onto the top of the sandwich.

The King of Supersized Sammies!

The Fool's Gold Loaf

The spirit of Elvis lives on with The Fool's Gold Loaf. The King's fave sammy makes
an ideal lunch for rockabillies and impersonators who love to keep the legend's
flame alive. Peanut butter, bacon, and grape jelly served on a massive loaf of crusty
bread—what die-hard Elvis fan wouldn't eat that up?

You'll Need:

- **1** 18-ounce package of bacon
- **1** 14-inch loaf of crusty Italian bread
- **1** 10-ounce jar of grape jelly
- **1** 18-ounce jar of creamy peanut butter

Instruments:

Nonstick skillet, bread knife, butter knife, spoon

Assembly:

1. Fry the bacon until crisp and allow to drain on paper towels.

2. Cut the loaf of bread in half lengthwise and spread the entire jar of grape jelly over the top half.

3. Spread three-quarters of the jar of peanut butter on the bottom half of the bread loaf and arrange the strips of bacon over top.

4. Spoon the remaining peanut butter over the bacon strips.

5. Slap both sides together when you're ready to eat it.

The Soulwich

Low carbing is so 2001. Rediscover all things bready and sweet with a 'wich based on the soul food favorite, chicken with waffles. The waffles are drenched in syrup and even the chicken doesn't get away unbreaded.

NOTE: For this photo, I used a premade chicken breast. But I've also prepared this dish uisng the below made-from-scratch recipe.

You'll Need:

⅓	cup fine breadcrumbs
½	teaspoon salt
	pepper to taste
	pinch of cumin
	pinch of dry mustard
1	five-ounce chicken breast
2	waffles, homemade or store-bought
1	large pimento olive
3–4	tablespoons maple syrup

Assembly:

1. If making the chicken from scratch, preheat oven to 400°F. Add breadcrumbs, salt, pepper, cumin, and dry mustard to Ziploc bag.

2. Place chicken breast inside bag and shake until completely coated.

3. Place chicken breast on baking sheet and cook in oven for 20 to 25 minutes until golden. Remove from oven and set aside to cool.

4. Toast store-bought waffles in toaster or make homemade following the recipe on page 45.

5. Place the first waffle on the plate, place chicken breast on waffle, and top with second waffle.

6. Pierce the olive with the toothpick and poke onto the top of the sandwich.

7. Pour the maple syrup over the sandwich so it spills over the top.

Instruments:

Large Ziploc bag, baking sheet, toaster, 1 toothpick

 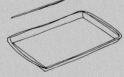

I poured my soul into this sandwich.

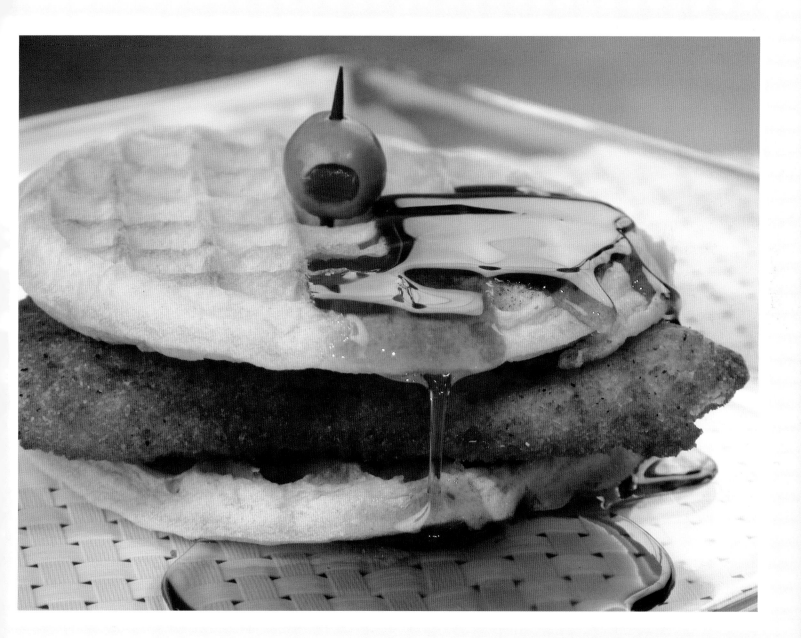

The Sumo Sandwich

This overstuffed heavyweight isn't just for sumo wrestlers. True, many of its ingredients are also found in a hearty, brothy hot pot dish called *nabe* (pronounced nah-bay)—a staple consumed by Sumo wrestlers to keep them bulked up for their matches—but anyone looking to fill up will enjoy grappling with this 'wich.

You'll Need:

- **8** ounces flank steak, sliced thinly
- **8** ounces chicken breast, sliced thinly
- **8** ounces salmon fillet, sliced thinly
- **6** tablespoons soy sauce
- **3** tablespoons white granulated sugar
- **½** cup safflower oil or canola oil
- **2** 14-ounce packages of udon noodles
- **3** ounces of daikon radish, sliced into thick matchstick-sized pieces
- **2** ounces of shiitake mushrooms, cleaned with ends of stems cut off
- **2** ounces of enoki mushrooms, cleaned with ends of stems cut off
- **1** tablespoon scallions, chopped

Instruments:

3 large Ziploc bags, chef's knife, chopping board, large skillet or wok, large spatula, baking sheet, large plate

Assembly:

1. Approximately two hours before constructing the sandwich, marinate the beef, chicken, and salmon in separate Ziploc bags with 2 tablespoons soy sauce and 1 tablespoon of sugar per bag.

2. Just before making the sandwich, chop the scallions, slice the daikon radish, and clean the mushrooms. Set aside.

3. Preheat oven to 200 ˚F.

4. Heat 3 tablespoons of safflower or canola oil in a large skillet or wok over medium-high heat.

5. Carefully place one package of udon noodles into the oil. The noodles will come out of the package stuck together. Do not spread them out or move them while they are browning, as they need to cook in one mass.

6. After 7–8 minutes, carefully flip the udon noodle mass with a large spatula and brown the other side for 7–8 minutes.

7. Remove noodles from oil with a spatula, allow to drain for a moment over paper towel and transfer to a baking sheet.

8. Repeat steps 5–7 with the second package of udon noodles.

9. Place the baking sheet in the oven to keep warm.

10. Remove excess oil from skillet or wok. Clean any debris and place back on stovetop. Heat 1 tablespoon of fresh oil over medium-high heat.

11. Remove beef, chicken and fish from the fridge. Stir fry each separately: The chicken will take about 9–10 minutes, the beef 7–8 minutes and the salmon 5–6 minutes. If the wok gets dry in between, simply add a teaspoon of oil. Set all aside on a large plate.

continued ➤

12. Stir fry each veggie separately, except for the scallions, which will be used as garnish. The daikon radish will take 7–8 minutes, the shiitake mushroom will take 4–5 minutes and the enoki mushroom 1–2 minutes. If the wok gets dry in between each veggie frying, simply add a half teaspoon of oil.

13. Remove warm noodles from oven and place one of the udon-noodle-turned-bread-slices on a plate.

14. Stack fillings in the following order: beef, chicken, salmon, shiitake mushrooms, enoki mushrooms, and daikon radish.

15. Top the sandwich with the second udon noodle bread slice and sprinkle scallions on the plate for garnish.

To fit it in your mouth, you may need to wrestle with it a bit.

The Crazy Canuck Sandwich

Many of you may not know that I hail from the land north of the 49th parallel. That's right—I'm a Canuck. So, to celebrate all things Canadian, here's an insanewich that contains beaver tails (no, not the real thing, silly, they're made out of fried dough), two types of bacon, and cheese curds. If you don't live in the north, and can't get your hands on some of these ingredients, don't worry. I provide easy-to-find substitutions.

You'll Need:

TO START YEAST:

¼ cup warm water

1 8-gram package of dry, quick-rise instant yeast

Pinch of white granulated sugar

Instruments:

2 large bowls, fork, large stock pot, small bowl, rolling pin, slotted spoon, spoon, baking sheet, nonstick skillet

FOR REST OF RECIPE:

⅓ cup warm milk

1 cup, **3** tablespoons white granulated sugar

½ teaspoon salt

½ teaspoon vanilla extract

1 egg

5 cups, **3** tablespoons, ¼ teaspoon canola oil

1½ cups all-purpose flour plus extra for dusting

2 teaspoons cinnamon

8 slices peameal bacon (or center-cut boneless pork loin, each slice approximately ¼ inch thick)

9 slices Canadian bacon

6 ounces white cheese curds (or white cheddar cheese, grated)

6 ounces yellow cheese curds (or yellow cheddar cheese, grated)

Assembly:

1. Preheat oven to 200°F.

2. In a large bowl, combine water, yeast, and a pinch of sugar. Stir with a fork and let rest for 3 minutes to allow yeast to dissolve.

3. Add milk, 3 tablespoons sugar, salt, vanilla, egg, 3 tablespoons oil, and flour to the bowl.

4. With your hands, combine all ingredients until they begin to stick together. Place dough onto a flour-dusted counter.

5. Knead the dough for about 5–6 minutes (don't overwork it, as that will make the final product tough) and place it into the second large bowl that's been coated with a ¼ teaspoon of oil.

6. Cover the bowl with a dish towel and keep it in a warm place for about 45 minutes.

7. After the dough has doubled in size, puncture it with your fingers to deflate.

8. Pour 5 cups of oil into a large stock pot and heat over medium heat.

9. Mix 1 cup of sugar and cinnamon in a small bowl and set aside.

10. Re-dust counter top with flour.

11. Pinch off a tennis ball-sized piece of dough and place it on your counter. With your hands, form it into a teardrop shape.

12. With a rolling pin, roll out the shape until it is about 8–9 inches long and about ¼-inch thick, maintaining the teardrop shape.

13. Repeat steps 11 and 12 two more times, reserving at least one tiny pea-sized piece of dough.

14. When the surface of the oil is shimmering, test the temperature of the oil with the pea-sized piece of dough. If the dough sizzles and puffs up immediately, the oil is ready.

15. Carefully ease one beaver tail into the oil. Fry for 3–4 minutes on one side, flip carefully with a slotted spoon, and fry for another 3–4 minutes. Remove beaver tail and allow to drain over paper towels for 10 seconds. Using a spoon, dust the tail with sugar and cinnamon mix while it's still hot.

16. Repeat step 15 two more times with the remaining tails.

17. Place the three beaver tails on a baking sheet and place sheet in oven to keep warm.

18. Fry the peameal and Canadian bacon in a skillet over medium heat and set aside.

19. Remove tails from oven and turn oven heat up to 450°F.

20. Remove one beaver tail from baking sheet and set aside.

21. On top of one of the tails remaining on the baking sheet, stack Canadian bacon and the white cheese curds. On the other tail, stack peameal bacon and yellow cheese curds.

22. Place the baking sheet back in the oven for 5–6 minutes or until curds start to become gooey. Remove from oven.

23. Place the Canadian-bacon-and-white-curd-topped tail on a plate. Place the peameal-and-yellow-curd-topped tail on top of the first tail.

24. Top the sandwich with the reserved beaver tail.

➤ *Goes well with a glass of maple syrup.*

The Pulmonary Clotwich with Flatline Mayo

Cardiologists, please look away. For the rest of you, get ready to enjoy one of the richest, creamiest 'wiches that's ever clogged an artery. With calorie-dense ingredients like liver paté, brie cheese, and mayonnaise, this French-inspired creation is a decadent treat that's sure to give the old ticker a workout. In fact, you may wanna check your pulse halfway through eating it.

You'll Need:

3 tablespoons mayo

25–30 drops red food coloring

3 slices of French brioche egg bread or challah, sliced thick

3 tablespoons butter (to spread on bread)

2 5-ounce packages of liver pâté (You will need to find a flat vacuum-packed-in-plastic variety, with each piece approximately $\frac{1}{2}$ inch thick by 4 inches long by 3 inches wide)

1 medium-sized wheel of brie (about 5 ounces brie, rind removed)

Instruments:

Bowl, small Ziploc bag, heart-shaped cookie cutter (3 inches top to bottom and 3½ inches left to right at the widest point), nonstick skillet, chef's knife, kitchen shears, long rectangular plate or platter, spatula

Assembly:

1. In a bowl, stir together mayo and red food coloring. Spoon mayo into a small Ziploc bag and refrigerate.

2. Using the cookie cutter, stamp out a heart shape from each slice of egg bread.

3. Heavily butter both sides of each slice of egg bread. Fry both sides of each slice in a nonstick skillet over medium-low heat until golden. Remove and set aside.

4. Using the cookie cutter, stamp a heart shape from each piece of liver pate.

5. Place the cookie cutter on a plate and spoon the brie into it, making sure to pack it down firmly. Gently lift the cookie cutter off.

6. Remove the bag of mayo from the fridge and squeeze its contents into the corner of the bag. Carefully twist the opposite end of the bag to pack it tightly.

7. Over the sink (because there might be a bit of spillage), snip a tiny $\frac{1}{16}$-inch corner from the bag.

8. Leaving about 3 or 4 inches of space on the left side of the platter to stack the sandwich, pipe a horizontal mayo line along the center of the plate about 2 inches long.

continued ➤

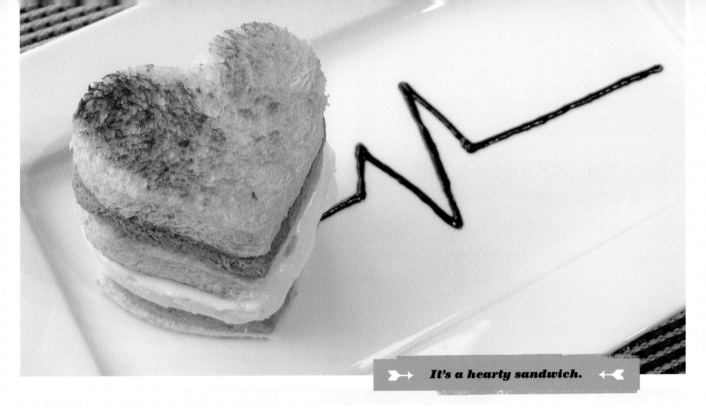

Step 4

Step 5

Step 6

9. Without breaking the line, continue piping a zigzag with one high peak, one low peak, and another high peak, in that order.

10. Without breaking the line, finish the flatline by piping a straight 6-inch horizontal line.

11. In the empty space on the platter, stack the sandwich as follows: one slice of bread, one slice of pâté, the brie cheese, the second slice of bread, the next slice of pâté, and the final slice of bread. You may wish to use a small spatula to finesse the delicate pâté and cheese hearts into place.

The Banana Split Trickwich

What follows isn't just a sandwich recipe, it's a recipe for one hilarious April Fools' gag. Take a closer peek. This dessert look-alike contains three scoops of mashed potato ice cream, bacon and chive sprinkles, gravy masquerading as chocolate sauce, and cherry tomatoes on top. Make it for your most gullible sweet-toothed friends and hope they don't hold a grudge!

You'll Need:

3 large white potatoes

1 tablespoon salt (½ for salting boiling water, ½ for seasoning potatoes)

4 slices bacon

1 tablespoon chives

½ cup warm milk

5 tablespoons butter

2 tablespoons flour

1 cup beef broth

4 ounces pre-grated yellow cheddar cheese

1 8-inch Italian sub bun

3 cherry tomatoes

Instruments:

Large stock pot, nonstick skillet, chef's knife, potato masher, saucepan, oval-shaped dish, bread knife, ice cream scoop, spoon

Assembly:

1. Boil potatoes in a large pot of salted water for 35–40 minutes.

2. Meanwhile, fry bacon in a nonstick skillet over medium heat, drain and chop. Set aside.

3. Chop chives finely and set aside.

4. When potatoes are fork tender, turn off stove, drain water, peel, and leave in pot. Add milk, 3 tablespoons of the butter and salt. With a potato masher, mash all ingredients until smooth and almost lump free. Cover pot.

5. For the gravy: In a small saucepan, over medium low heat, melt remaining 2 tablespoons of butter, add 2 tablespoons of flour and mix thoroughly to make a roux. Cook for 3 minutes until blond.

6. Add beef broth and continue stirring for another five minutes or until gravy becomes thick. Turn heat to low and stir occasionally to keep skin from forming.

7. Make a bed of grated cheese in an oval-shaped dish.

8. Slice the bun in half lengthwise and place each half in the oval plate lengthwise, leaving space for the mashed potato scoops in between the bun halves.

9. With an ice cream scoop, place three scoops of mashed potato side by side in between the bun halves.

10. Sprinkle the bacon bits and chives on top of the mashed potato scoops, drizzle streams of gravy with a spoon, and add one cherry tomato on top of each scoop.

Don't Mess with Texwich!

A big ol' saddle-sized sammy boasting Texas toast shaped like the longhorn state itself deserves its own slogan: "Everything's Bigger in Texwich!" That's right, there's nothing small or subtle about this honking hoagie.

You'll Need:

- **7** slices Texas toast bread
- **2** tablespoons mayo
- **½** teaspoon ancho chile powder
- **2** tablespoons olive oil
- **½** medium Spanish onion, sliced
- **½** yellow bell pepper, sliced
- **½** orange bell pepper, sliced
  - salt and pepper to taste
- **1** 10-ounce rib eye steak
- **1** slice pepper jack cheese
- **2** tablespoons sour cream
- **2** tablespoons Texas-style BBQ sauce
- **1** tablespoon picante sauce
- **3–4** tablespoons butter

Instruments:

Grill pan, small bowl, plastic wrap, nonstick skillet, oven mitts, tongs, toaster

Assembly:

1. Using the template provided for this recipe and the bread-carving technique described on page 17, cut out the shape required for this sandwich from one slice of Texas toast bread (Texas state).

2. Turn oven to broil and place your cast iron grill pan inside close to the top, for at least 10 minutes, to get scorching hot.

3. Meanwhile, in a small bowl, stir together mayo and ancho chile powder. Cover with plastic wrap and refrigerate.

4. In a nonstick skillet, over medium heat, add 1 tablespoon olive oil. Add onions and bell peppers. Season with salt and pepper and cook for 7–8 minutes or until caramelized. Remove from heat.

5. Coat both sides of the ribeye steak with 1 tablespoon of olive oil and season with salt and pepper.

6. Carefully remove grill pan from oven with oven mitts and place steak on grill pan.

7. Place the grill pan back in the oven for 3–4 minutes, remove the pan again, flip the steak with the tongs, and let cook for another 3–4 minutes. For a 1-inch steak 3–4 minutes per side will yield medium-rare doneness. Remove the steak from the oven and take it off the grill pan to rest for a few minutes.

8. Toast two of the regular slices of Texas toast bread as well as the slice that you carved into the shape of Texas state.

9. Lay one regular slice of toasted Texas bread on a plate.

10. Lay the slice of pepper jack cheese on top and then spoon on the ancho mayo.

continued ➤

11. Spread the onion and bell pepper mixture over the mayo.

12. Add the second regular slice of toasted Texas bread on top and dollop with sour cream.

13. Place the steak on top of the sour cream and spread Texas BBQ sauce and picante sauce over it. Top the creation with the slice that you carved into the shape of Texas state.

14. Toast four more slices of regular Texas toast bread, butter heavily and serve alongside the Texwich.

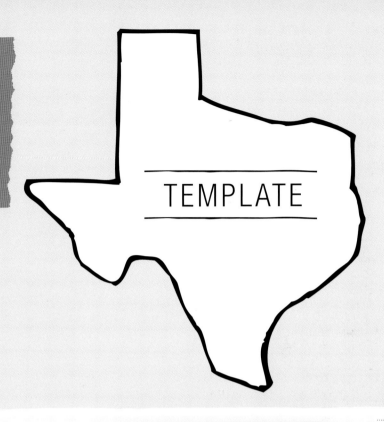

TEMPLATE

So what is Texas toast?

Contrary to what you might think, it doesn't come already toasted. Often square in shape, a loaf of Texas toast bread is sold presliced, with its slices two times as thick as most conventional breads. It's often served toasted and buttered and it's perfect for when you wanna stack a huge sammy!

>→ *The Lone Star Sandwich* ←<

The Fish 'N' Chipwich

In the mega-caloric realm of fatty 'wiches, there aren't many that can rival this English-inspired fish 'n' chip sandwich. Almost everything's deep-fried here except for the newspaper boat (but believe me, I was tempted!).

You'll Need:

- **¾** cup flour
- **1** egg
- **½** cup milk
    salt and pepper to taste
- **2** Yukon gold potatoes
- **2** tablespoons mayo
- **1** tablespoon green relish
- **1** lemon
- **5** cups corn oil
- **1** 6-ounce tilapia fillet (I cut the fillet in half down the centerline and used the thicker half)
    bottom half of 8-inch baguette

Instruments:

Large bowl, whisk, chef's knife, large stock pot, small bowl, slotted spoon, tongs, UK flag for decoration, newspaper boat

Assembly:

1. For the batter: In the large bowl, combine flour, egg, milk, salt and pepper to taste and whisk until all lumps are gone. Set aside.

2. Cut potatoes into French fries about ¼-inch thick. Place in a pot with plenty of water and bring water to a boil. Par boil potatoes for about 7–8 minutes. They will only be partially cooked at this point.

3. Remove pot from stove, drain potatoes; let them cool and dry on paper towel.

4. For the tartar sauce: In the small bowl, mix mayo with relish and squeeze of lemon.

5. Prep for deep frying: In a large stock pot, heat oil over medium-high heat until shimmering. To test oil, drop in a tiny bit of batter. If it sizzles and rises immediately, the oil is ready.

6. Ease fries into oil carefully. Cook in oil for 5–6 minutes or until golden.

7. Remove fries from oil with a slotted spoon and drain over paper towel. Season with salt while still hot.

8. Holding the fish fillet by one end with a pair of tongs, dip fish into batter and then gently ease it into the oil, laying it away from your body to avoid splatters.

9. Fry each side for 3–4 minutes or until golden. Remove fish from oil and allow to drain on paper towel. Season with salt while still hot.

10. Spread tartar sauce on the baguette half.

11. Place fries on the baguette.

12. Place the fish on top of the fries.

13. Stick UK flag into the fish and serve in newspaper boat with a lemon wedge.

There's weight gain on the horizon!

shape
wiches

7

If you're reeling (and feeling a bit plump) after all those fatty 'wiches, you're most likely suffering from a serious food hangover. Not to worry, there are plenty of waist-friendly insanewiches that'll get you back on track. These Shapewiches are a wise choice when the scale's giving you grief. If Jared Fogle got slim with sandwiches, so can you!

Slimwiches

Measurements not what they used to be? Sounds like it's time to make yourself one of these shapely sandwiches instead of reaching for that bag of chips. They are healthy sources of protein and carbs, so you'll feel guilt-free about having one after your aerobics or yoga class. Add them to your routine and watch your tummy retreat.

You'll Need:

FOR TWO SLIMWICHES:

- **6** ounces low-fat cottage cheese
  pepper to taste
- **1** tablespoon raisins
- **4** slices multigrain bread
- **3** radishes, sliced
- **1** apple, sliced
- **1** cucumber
- **1** large carrot (minimum length 9 inches)

Instruments:

2 small bowls, chef's knife, vegetable peeler

Assembly:

1. In one bowl, mix 3 ounces of cottage cheese with pepper to taste. In another bowl, mix 3 ounces of cottage cheese with raisins.

2. Using the template provided with this recipe and the bread-carving technique described on page 17, cut out the shape required for this sandwich (hourglass figure).

3. On top of one slice, layer the sliced radishes and the peppery cottage cheese. On a second slice, layer the sliced apples and the raisin cottage cheese. Top each sandwich with the remaining slices of bread.

4. With a vegetable peeler, peel off two long, thin strips of skin from the cucumber.

5. Repeat step 4 with large carrot.

6. With the chef's knife, cut small, ¼-inch thick pieces from the cucumber strips.

7. For each sandwich, carefully slide one carrot slice "belt" underneath the sandwich until you get to the waist, then wrap one side around the waist, and tuck the tip of the carrot belt underneath the sandwich's waist to keep it secure.

8. Space the cucumber pieces about ½-inch apart on top of the carrot belt to represent units of measure.

TEMPLATE

*The sandwiches that'll cinch
your weight-loss success!*

It's a huge lunch...if you're a Smurf.

Cutecumber 'Wich

You may need to squint a tad to make out the itty-bitty fillings in this downsized 'wich. Two mini cucumber slices are divided by a slice of yellow cherry tomato, tiny basil leaves, and a teaspoon of mint-infused yogurt. And to wash it all down: a thimble full of sparkling water. Talk about small portions!

You'll Need:

1 small Kirby cucumber

1 yellow cherry tomato

1 teaspoon yogurt

1 small mint leaf, chopped

2 small basil leaves

1 thimble full of sparkling water

Assembly:

1. Slice two ¼-inch rounds from the cucumber.

2. Slice one ½-inch round from the yellow cherry tomato.

3. In a small bowl, mix the yogurt and mint.

4. To assemble, stack the cucumber slice, yellow cherry tomato slice, the two basil leaves, the yogurt mix, and second cucumber slice.

5. Poke a toothpick through the sandwich and serve with a thimble of sparkling water.

Instruments:

Chef's knife, bowl, toothpick, thimble

These wraps have been scaled down for dieters.

Wee Wittle Wraps

You don't want to resort to pant styles with elastic waistbands, right? Then have one of these lightweights to help you count calories. Each one is scarcely larger than your thumb, which means you can ditch those track pants you picked up at the plus size or big 'n' tall store.

You'll Need:

FOR FIVE WRAPS:

5 small whole wheat wraps

10 slices tofu deli meat

2½ teaspoons Dijon mustard

5 leafy green lettuce leaves

2½ ounces bean sprouts

Instruments:

4-inch diameter round cookie cutter, 3-inch diameter round cookie cutter

Assembly:

1. Using the 4-inch diameter round cookie cutter, stamp out one round from each whole wheat wrap slice.

2. Stack two slices of tofu deli meat, and using the 3-inch diameter round cookie cutter, stamp rounds from the two stacked slices.

3. Repeat step 2 four more times.

4. Assemble the wraps in the following way: lay the wraps down, spread ½ teaspoon Dijon mustard on each, stack two slices of tofu deli meat on each, then one leaf of lettuce and ½ ounce sprouts.

5. Roll each wrap as tightly as possible.

Dumbbell Diet 'Wich

Putting together this one will serve as a harsh reminder: You've gotta hit the gym hard if you wanna lose that flab! You remember that place, right? Bench presses, pushups, curls–every rep counts! Quit being a dumbbell about your fitness goals and fuel your next workout with this good-for-you 'wich.

You'll Need:

- **1** package firm tofu
- **1** teaspoon light olive oil
- **4** slices flax seed bread
- **4** slices of tofu cheese
- **1** thick breadstick

Instruments:

2½-inch round cookie cutter, apple corer

Assembly:

1. Preheat oven to 375°F.

2. From the package of firm tofu, slice two ½-inch slices and lightly coat in oil.

3. Bake tofu slices in oven for 12–15 minutes or until they begin to brown. Remove from oven and allow to cool to room temperature.

4. With the round cookie cutter, stamp out one round from each of the slices of bread and from the two slices of tofu cheese. Then stamp one round from each of the firm tofu slices.

5. With the apple corer, stamp a small hole out of the center of each bread slice, tofu cheese, and firm tofu round.

6. Carefully slide one bread round, one slice of cheese, one firm tofu slice, and a second bread round onto one side of the breadstick. Leave about ½-inch tip of the breadstick sticking out.

7. Repeat step 6 on the other side of the breadstick with the remaining ingredients in the same order.

Curl sandwich to mouth for toned biceps.

The Beaming Carrot Top Sandwich

Dieting won't suck when your diet food looks back at you with a big red peppery smile. Forget the wheat grass shake (Yuck! That'll put a frown on your face) and make this happy hummus sandwich for lunch instead. It'll be smiles all round.

You'll Need:

- **½** cup canned chickpeas, drained
- **2** tablespoons tahini
- **2** tablespoons lemon juice
- **1** garlic clove
- salt and pepper to taste
- **½** teaspoon cumin
- **1** teaspoon olive oil
- **2** slices whole wheat bread
- **2** large cremini mushrooms, cleaned and sliced
- **½** red bell pepper, sliced
- **½** cherry tomato
- **2** edamame beans
- **1** ounce shredded or grated carrots

Assembly:

1. For the hummus: Add canned chickpeas, tahini, lemon juice, garlic, salt, pepper, cumin, and olive oil to a food processor. Pulse until smooth and set aside.

2. With the round cookie cutter, stamp out rounds from the two slices of bread.

3. Lay one of the slices on a plate and spread the hummus over top.

4. Layer the mushroom slices and red bell pepper slices over the hummus (reserve one red bell pepper slice for the mouth).

5. Cover with second slice of bread.

6. Place the reserved red bell pepper slice on top as the smiling mouth, cherry tomato half as the nose, and edamame beans as the two eyes.

7. Arrange strands of carrot facing upwards as carrot top hair. I used store-bought shredded carrots because they are drier and won't make the bread as soggy, but you can grate your own if you wish.

Instruments:

Chef's knife, food processor, 4-inch diameter round cookie cutter

TEMPLATE

 Feed your kid some Brussels with muscles!

The No-Fuss Brussels Sandwich

True Fact: Brussels sprouts make every kid's top-ten list of most despised foods. So to make 'em more appealing, give this fun but healthy superhero insanewich a shot. It's rippling with vitamins and minerals from head to torso.

You'll Need:

- **2** slices sunflower and walnut bread
- **3** Brussels sprouts
  Salt to taste
- **2** carrots
- **1** teaspoon low-fat mayo
- **1** shallot, sliced

Instruments:

Bread knife, small pot, chef's knife, spoon

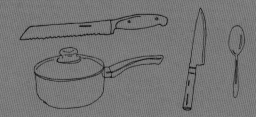

Assembly:

1. Using the template provided in this recipe and the bread-carving technique described on page 17, cut out the shape required for this sandwich (torso).

2. Boil three Brussels sprouts in salted water for 7–8 minutes or until fork tender.

3. Slice two of them thinly and reserve one whole. Slice two carrots on the bias. Choose six slices, making sure that two are large, two are medium-sized, and two are small.

4. Spoon the mayo on one slice of bread. Layer on the shallots and Brussels sprouts. Top the sandwich with the second slice of bread.

5. Place the reserved sprout at the top of the sandwich as its head.

6. Place the larger carrot slices as shoulders, medium slices as biceps, and small slices as hands.

Don't Eat Like A Bird!

I made this sandwich to remind you that eating too little isn't a good way to keep fit. You gotta fuel yourself properly to succeed. A word of advice: After making this one, eat it immediately. Don't hang it on your porch or the big oak tree, as you will attract an inordinate number of feathered friends.

You'll Need:

2 slices dark rye bread

2 slices light rye bread with caraway seeds

1 pretzel stick

½ cooked chicken breast, chopped fine

1½ tablespoons nonfat mayo

1 tablespoon parsley

salt and pepper to taste

Instruments:

Apple corer, bowl, spoon

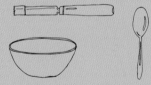

Assembly:

1. Using the templates provided for this recipe and the bread-carving technique on page 17, cut out the bread shapes required for this sandwich from the dark rye and light rye (birdhouse). When you carve out the roof pieces from the two slices of dark rye, there will be excess bread. Reserve this excess.

2. Using the apple corer, stamp a hole into one of the light rye house base slices of bread. Make sure to leave some space beneath the hole, where the pretzel stick will go.

3. Using the apple corer, stamp one round out of the excess bread that was cut away from one of the slices of dark rye. Reserve this round.

4. In a bowl, mix chicken, nonfat mayo, parsley, salt, and pepper.

5. Lay the first light rye house base slice down (the one without the hole) and place one dark rye roof slice on top so they are butting up against each other (roof over house base).

6. Spoon the chicken salad on top of the first roof-and-house layer.

7. Place the second roof-and-house slices on top of the chicken salad.

8. Stick the pretzel into the sandwich right below the hole.

9. Place the reserved dark rye round down into the hole.

This sandwich is not for the birds!

TEMPLATES

The Healthy Cakewich

This may be the world's first birthday cake that'll help you shed pounds and not gain 'em. With low-fat and healthy ingredients, it allows you to get a year older without getting a pound heavier.

You'll Need:

- **1** small sweet potato
- **1** tablespoon salt
- **3** slices multigrain bread
- **8** slices extra-lean chicken deli slices

Instruments:

Saucepan, potato masher, steak knife, chef's knife, large Ziploc bag, kitchen shears, birthday candle

Assembly:

1. Boil a small sweet potato in a saucepan with salted water, drain, and let cool slightly before peeling. Leave sweet potato in saucepan and, with potato masher, mash until soft.

2. Using the template provided in this recipe and the bread-carving technique described on page 17, cut the shape required for this sandwich (cake shape) out of the bread slices.

3. Divide the slices of chicken deli meat into two even piles.

4. Using the template provided in this recipe and the bread-carving technique (it works on deli slices too!) described on page 17, cut the shape required for this sandwich (cake shape) out of the slices of each pile of chicken deli slices (use chef's knife for deli slices).

5. Stack as follows: slice of bread, first pile of chicken deli slices, second bread slice, second pile of chicken deli slices, third slice of bread.

6. Place mashed sweet potato in a large Ziploc bag and squeeze all contents tightly in one corner.

7. Twist the back end of the bag and cut off a small ½-inch corner.

8. Pipe sweet potato frosting along the edge of the top slice of bread

9. Insert candle into sandwich and light.

Make a 'wich and blow out the candle!

TEMPLATE

Chapter Eight

OMG
wiches

And then there are some insanewiches that are just plain bizarre. They look really funny or make use of some pretty strange (but tasty) ingredient combos. Of course, I'm talking about OMGwiches. These ones are so weird they'll leave you scratching your head trying to figure out what the heck just happened!

What The Breadwich?

You're probably wondering what on earth I used as the bread. I'll give you three guesses:
Nope, it's not a dinner roll. Uh-uh, not a hamburger bun. Negative, they ain't muffin tops.
Those are two grilled Portobello mushrooms. Thanks for playing!

You'll Need:

- **2** large Portobello mushroom caps, stems removed
- **2** tablespoons olive oil

  salt and pepper to taste
- **1** slice Swiss cheese
- **3** slices turkey breast (deli meat)
- **1** Boston lettuce leaf
- **2** chive strands

Assembly:

1. Preheat grill pan on stovetop over medium heat.
2. Lightly coat both sides of each Portobello cap with olive oil and season with salt and pepper.
3. Grill both caps on both sides for about 3–4 minutes per side.
4. Place one cap on the plate bottom side up.
5. Layer on the Swiss cheese, turkey breast slices, and lettuce and top with second mushroom cap.
6. Add chives for garnish.

Instruments:

Grill pan, tongs

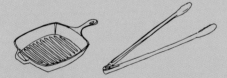

We're Turning Chocolese, I Really Think So...

Chocolese may sound like a foreign tongue, but it's actually the language you'll mysteriously start speaking after you taste this delish combination of chocolate and cheese. Skip the books and classes—from now on language lessons start at the lunch table.

You'll Need:

1 cup water

3 ounces of your preferred dark or milk chocolate

1 large slice light rye bread

2 slices Swiss cheese

Instruments:

Saucepan, stainless steel bowl, wooden spoon, baking sheet

Assembly:

1. Preheat oven to 350°F.

2. Pour water into a saucepan and bring to a very gentle boil over low heat.

3. Place the bowl over the saucepan to create a double boiler so that the chocolate doesn't burn.

4. Add chocolate to the bowl and stir until melted. Stir frequently so it doesn't clump.

5. Put bread slice on a baking sheet and lay slices of cheese over top.

6. Place in oven for 3 minutes or until cheese gets oozy.

7. Remove from oven and drizzle with melted chocolate.

The Banaconator

Everything's better with bacon. It's the universal truth that inspired this eclectic concoction. Chocolate and bananas—sure, that's tasty. But what happens when bacon joins the show? Porky, crispy, sweet 'n' salty perfection, that's what!

You'll Need:

- **4** slices of bacon
- **1** cup water
- **3** ounces of your preferred dark or milk chocolate
- **1** medium-sized banana
- **2** slices white bread

Instruments:

Nonstick skillet, saucepan, stainless steel bowl, wooden spoon, chef's knife, toaster

Assembly:

1. Fry bacon until crisp and let it drain on paper towel.
2. Pour water into a saucepan and bring to a very gentle boil over low heat.
3. Place the bowl over the saucepan to create a double boiler so that the chocolate doesn't burn.
4. Add chocolate to the bowl and stir until melted. Stir frequently so it doesn't clump.
5. Slice the banana into thin slices.
6. Toast the bread.
7. Place one slice of bread on a plate and layer the banana and bacon slices on bread. Drizzle the melted chocolate over top.
8. Top sandwich with second slice of bread.

Bacon + Anything = Awesome!

Cordless Mousewich with USB Cheesestick

Ever been surfing the Web, pointing and clicking, when suddenly four minutes turns into four hours? If so, feast your bleary eyes on this cordless treat. It's about time you peeled your hiney from that chair, gave your eyes a break, and had a snack already!

You'll Need:

- **1** small computer mouse-shaped dinner roll
- **1** 6-ounce hamsteak (½ inch thick)
- **1** hotdog
- **½** ounce yellow cheddar (block, not presliced)
- **⅛** ounce white cheddar (block, not presliced)

Instruments:

Bread knife, chef's knife, steak knife, mouse pad, ruler, chopping board

Assembly:

1. With your bread knife, cut a small 90° angle cavity out of the top third of the dinner roll. The cavity should be about ½ inch deep (vertically) from the top of the bun and 1½ inches deep (horizontally) from the front.

2. Cut a ¼-inch slice from the bottom of the dinner roll. This will allow the sandwich to sit flat and give it a realistic mouse-like appearance.

3. Cut a 1½-inch by 2½-inch rectangle out of the hamsteak. This will be used to make the right- and left-click buttons.

4. Place the rectangle inside the 90° cavity.

5. With your chef's knife, slowly and carefully carve the ham, removing the excess until it is contoured with the bread. The edge of the bun will guide you.

6. After you shave away the excess, you will be left with a piece of ham that fits perfectly into the 90° angle space.

7. Remove the carved ham and cut it in half to form two buttons. Then from each button, cut out a small, ¼-inch by ½-inch, 90° segment as shown.

8. Slice a small ¼-inch thick cross-section from the hotdog. Slice approximately one-third off this slice to form the scroll wheel.

9. Using the steak knife, cut a ¼-inch by ¼-inch square from the top of the bun as shown.

10. Once you have cut the square, it's very easy to just pull it out with your fingers.

11. Place the right- and left-click ham buttons back in the cavity.

continued ➤→

12. Squeeze the hotdog scroll wheel in between them.

13. For the cheesy USB stick: Cut a yellow cheddar cheesestick about 2 inches long by about ¼ inch thick. Then cut a smaller ⅛ inch by ⅛ inch cube from the white cheddar. Lay them beside each other to form a realistic-looking cheese USB stick.

Right-click options: Save as snack; Add to lunch favorites; Eat source.

Step 1

Step 4   **Step 5**   **Step 6**   **Step 7**

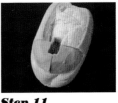

Step 8   **Step 9**   **Step 10**   **Step 11**   **Step 12**

The 'Stachewich

The mustache has made a comeback, and it ain't just hipsters sporting 'em! There's a whole sandwich crowd getting in on the trend. Take Mr. Stachewich here. He's got a hairy upper lip that'd make Magnum PI or Salvador Dalí jealous!

You'll Need:

- **1** long slice Italian bread cut from a large, round Calabrese-style loaf
- **2** slices bologna
- **6** chickpeas
- **1** small pimento olive
- **2** cherry tomatoes
- **2** sprigs dill
- **2** slices Genoa salami
- **1** large pimento olive
- **1** pretzel stick

Instruments:

bread knife, toothpick

Assembly:

1. Cut the slice of bread in half and place one half on plate.
2. Place two slices of bologna on top of bread
3. Lift the top slice of bologna slightly, and line up the six chickpea teeth in between the two slices.
4. Place the small pimento olive nose on the top slice of bologna.
5. Place the two cherry tomato eyes slightly behind either side of the nose.
6. Place one sprig of dill under either side of the nose.
7. Place the second half of bread on top of the eyes so that it slopes downward toward the back end of the sandwich.
8. Place one slice of Genoa salami on top of the sandwich.
9. Roll the other slice of salami into a cylinder with your hands.
10. Thread a toothpick through the overlapping salami ends as shown on next page.
11. Affix the cylinder standing up so that the toothpick is poking into the first slice of salami and top slice of bread.
12. Empty the large olive of its pimento and poke it in the side with the pretzel.
13. Place pretzel into the side of the sandwich's mouth to form the pipe.

Step 9

Step 10

Step 11

East Meets Westdog

If you order insanewich maki rolls at your favorite sushi bar, don't look surprised when you get these nori-wrapped hot dogs! The combo sounds odd, but trust me, it's a snack and an adventure rolled into one.

You'll Need

- **2** hot dogs
- **2** sheets of nori (Japanese seaweed, each sheet 7½ by 8 inches)
- **2** hot dog buns
  dabs of water
- **½** teaspoon wasabi
- **1** teaspoon ketchup
- **1** tablespoon pickled ginger

Instruments:

Small pot, sushi mat, sheet of plastic wrap, chopping board, chef's knife

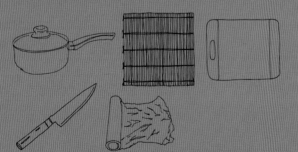

Assembly:

1. Boil hot dogs for 5 minutes, drain pot, set dogs aside to cool.
2. Place sushi mat on counter and top with enough plastic wrap to cover mat.
3. Place sheet of nori on plastic wrap.
4. Place one hot dog bun on top of nori, then place one hot dog inside bun.
5. Lift sushi mat and roll nori with hot dog "maki" inside.
6. Continue rolling and just before you finish, dab a little bit of water on the edge of the nori sheet with your finger to seal the roll.
7. Flip back the mat and remove the sheet of plastic wrap from the nori-wrapped hot dog.
8. Repeat steps 2–7 above to make the second hot dog maki.
9. Place both rolls on a chopping board and cut the tip ends from each with the chef's knife. Discard.
10. Next, cut each roll in half to form four even maki.
11. Arrange the rolls on a plate facing up.
12. Put wasabi, ketchup, and ginger onto plate next to maki.

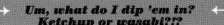
Um, what do I dip 'em in?
Ketchup or wasabi?!?

Ahoy! I've been strandwiched for weeks!

Lost At Seawich

If this lost-at-sea sammy could send you an SOS, here's what it'd say: "Mayday! I've been floating on this breadstick raft tied together with chives for ages. Please, send help. I promise I will make a tasty snack when I hit dry land!"

You'll Need:

- **3** slices dark party rye bread
- **4** ounces presliced smoked salmon
- **14** chives
- **8** breadsticks
- **1** tortilla chip
- **1** teaspoon bean dip

Instruments:

Round 2-inch diameter cookie cutter, kitchen shears, large skewer, black edible marker

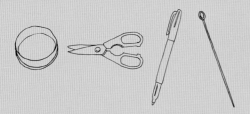

Assembly:

1. Using the cookie cutter, stamp one round from each slice of dark party rye bread.

2. Using the cookie cutter, stamp two rounds out of the smoked salmon.

3. Tie one chive on each end of seven of the breadsticks. Cut excess chive with kitchen shears. Reserve one breadstick.

4. Arrange the seven chive-wrapped breadsticks beside one another. Make sure they are slightly uneven to look like a realistic raft.

5. Assemble the rye and salmon rounds as follows: one slice rye, smoked salmon, next slice rye, smoked salmon, last slice rye. Make sure they are perfectly aligned.

6. Using the large skewer, poke a hole down through the center of the sandwich.

7. Using the edible marker, write "Help!" on the tortilla chip.

8. Dab the bean dip on the back of the tortilla chip and "glue" the chip to the top of the reserved breadstick.

9. Place this "flagpole" in the freezer for a few minutes, so the bean dip will set.

10. Remove flagpole from freezer and poke it into the hole you made in the sandwich.

11. Carefully place the sandwich on the raft.

Egghead Salad Sandwich

You're lookin' at arguably the brainiest sandwich in the book. This keener scored remarkably high on the flavor exam, aced the SATwiches and even got on the Dean's lunch list. What else would you expect from an eggheaded genius?

You'll Need:

2 slices white bread

2 eggs, hardboiled, peeled

1 tablespoon mayonnaise

½ small tomato

3 basil leaves

salt and pepper to taste

4 ounces egg whites (from carton)

15–20 drops green food coloring

1 tablespoon olive oil

½ red bell pepper

Instruments:

Food processor, bowl, fork, nonstick skillet, spoon, chef's knife, steak knife

Assembly:

1. Using the template provided and the bread-carving technique described on page 17, cut out the shape required for this sandwich (head side-profile). Reserve the excess white bread.

2. Place the whole boiled eggs in a food processor, add mayo, tomato, basil leaves, salt, and pepper. Pulse until almost fine. Set aside.

3. In a bowl, mix egg whites and green food coloring with a fork until fully incorporated.

4. Add olive oil to nonstick skillet over medium heat.

5. Add green egg mixture to skillet and scramble until cooked.

6. Lay one slice of bread down on a plate and spoon egg salad mixture over top.

7. Top the sandwich with the second slice of bread.

8. Skin the half red bell pepper as described on page 19 and cut a small triangle using the chef's knife. Place it on top of the second slice of bread as Egghead's eye.

9. With a spoon arrange the green egg mixture over the top of the head as hair, and if possible, shape some of the mixture into a sideburn. With the excess reserved white bread, carve out a small kidney bean-shaped piece using a steak knife. Place it to the right of the sideburn as the ear.

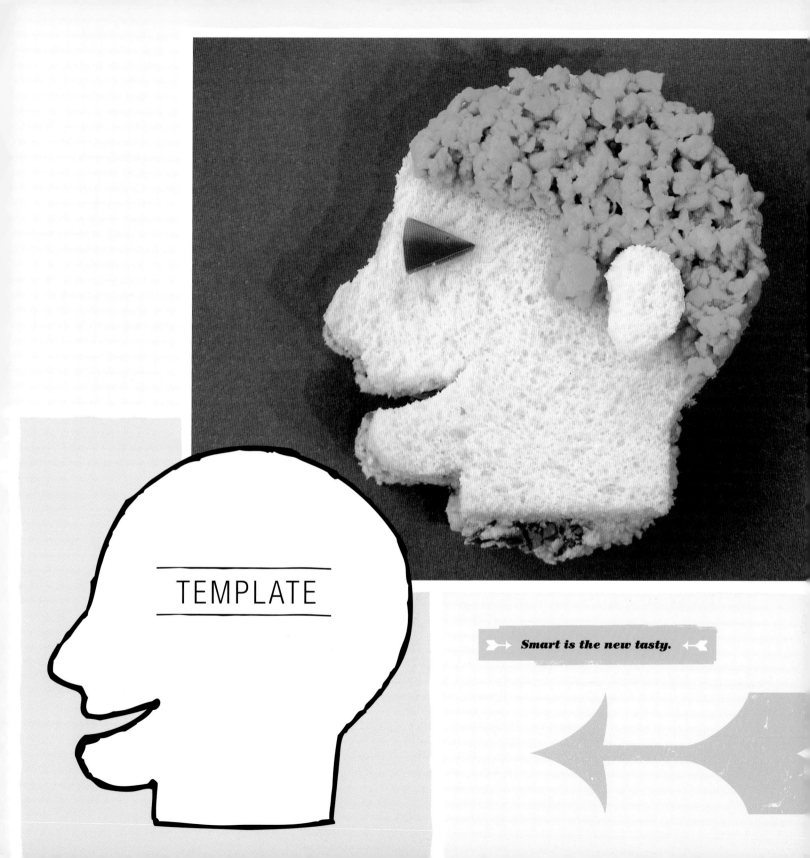

TEMPLATE

Smart is the new tasty.

Flatbread Fred

You're probably wondering, Why the long face? Fred's in the dumps 'cause that special somewich hasn't come along yet. Don't fret, Fred, you've got goat cheese and red pepper jelly on thin, savory flatbread, so it's only a matter of time before your true sandwich love catches wind.

Cheer up Fred, there's plenty of 'wich in the sea.

You'll Need:

- **2** pieces long, thin oval flatbread
- **4** ounces goat cheese
- **3** tablespoons red pepper jelly
- **½** red bell pepper
- **2** slices from a large radish
- **2** slices from a carrot
- **1** asparagus tip
- **1** sliver cut from a yellow bell pepper

Instruments:

Spoon, chef's knife

Assembly:

1. Lay the first flatbread slice down and spread with goat cheese and red pepper jelly.

2. Lay second flatbread slice on top.

3. Cut two strips from the red bell pepper about ½ inch by 1½ inches in size.

4. Place them near the top of the second flatbread slice as Fred's eyebrows. Make sure they're slanted to give him a sad expression.

5. Cut two slices from the radish and place them under the eyebrows as the whites of Fred's eyes.

6. Cut two slices from the carrot and place them inside the radish slices as pupils looking downward and to the left.

7. Cut the tip from the asparagus, microwave it for 45 seconds, and place it as the nose, tip facing down.

8. Cut one sliver from the yellow bell pepper and place it as the frown so the ends are facing down.

Catch O' The Daywich

If you went fishing and only caught a boot, make this 'wich to keep from feeling like you got totally skunked. Who needs a shore lunch when you can have flavored tuna on white? But keep in mind that if you share it with friends, you won't be able to tell fish tales about how big that catch was.

Option: Feel free to use 1 small can of your favorite preflavored tuna. If you do, you can skip step 1 below.

You'll Need:

½ can tuna

1 tablespoon olive oil

squeeze of lemon

¼ teaspoon paprika

salt and pepper to taste

2 slices white bread

1 ⅛ inch thick round slice of carrot (cut from close to the tip end)

Assembly:

1. In a bowl, mix tuna, oil, lemon, paprika, salt, and pepper.

2. Using the cookie cutter, stamp a fish shape out of each slice of bread.

3. Spoon tuna mixture on top of one bread slice and top with the second.

4. Place carrot slice on top of sandwich as the fish eye.

Warning: If you use a real fishing hook for decorative purposes when making this sandwich, definitely yank it out before eating!

Instruments:

Bowl, fork, fish-shaped cookie cutter (3 inches from nose to tail, 1½ inches from top to bottom), spoon

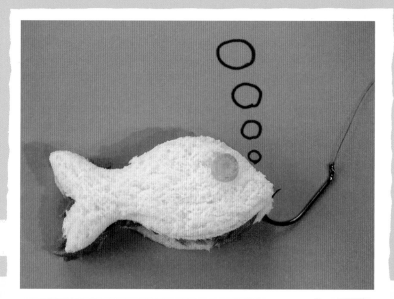

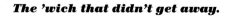

➡ ***The 'wich that didn't get away.***

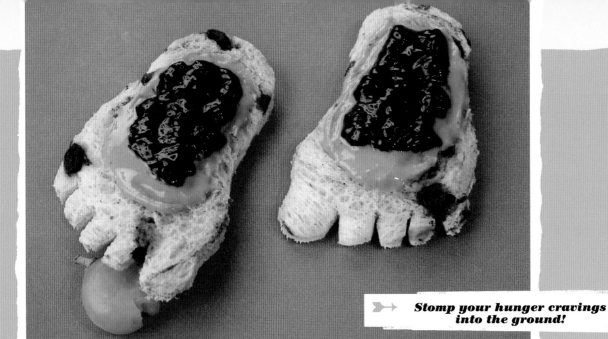

Stomp your hunger cravings
into the ground!

Foot Stompwiches

Wine lovers will appreciate a snack that celebrates the glorious grape—especially one
that includes grape jelly and foot-shaped raisin bread stomping a fresh green grape.
Who needs finger sandwiches when you can have foot stompwiches?

You'll Need:

2 slices raisin bread

2 tablespoons peanut butter

2 heaping teaspoons grape jam

1 grape

Instruments:

Foot-shaped cookie cutter (3¾ inches from big
toe to heel, 2¼ inches from side to side at widest
point), spoon

Assembly:

1. Using the cookie cutter, stamp a left foot shape out of one slice of raisin
   bread.

2. Flip the cookie cutter and stamp a right foot shape from the second
   slice of raisin bread.

3. Using a spoon, spread each foot with 1 tablespoon of peanut butter
   and 1 heaping teaspoon of grape jam on top of the peanut butter.

4. Smoosh a grape between your fingers and place it under the big toe of
   one foot.

STACK THE ODDWICHES IN YOUR FAVOR

It's happened to all of us at one point or another: You're so hungry, you slap your sandwich together haphazardly, and when you take a bite, the fillings shoot out faster than you can say ham and cheese on rye! To prevent this tragedy, here are some foolproof stacking tips.

THE BASE

Without a solid base, your sandwich will lean like the Tower of Pisa or topple over like you just lost at Jenga®. So make sure that the first slice (bread or otherwise) that you lay down is even in thickness. This "anchor slice," as I call it, should create a level surface for all other ingredients. Even a small variation in the thickness of the anchor slice could create an unlevel, inconsistent base.

What causes an uneven anchor slice? Sometimes when you freeze store-bought bread, it warps and its thickness becomes irregular. If you're going to freeze bread, take it out of the original bag and lay slices flat in a large Ziploc bag. That way, you're not freezing the slices standing up, which could cause them to droop and buckle when thawed.

Sloppy bread-slicing technique is another reason you'll end up with a wonky anchor slice. If you've made your own bread or bought a fresh, unsliced loaf, make sure to let it cool to room temperature before slicing it; otherwise you run the risk of flattening it with your bread knife.

GET STACKING

Once you've got your anchor slice down, the way you stack ingredients is crucial to preventing sliding and toppling. My general rule of thumb is "Build Your Sandwich Even, Steven." Start by minding the thickness of each ingredient before layering. Make sure that ingredients aren't off to one side (unless it's for effect), and cut veggies—like tomatoes and cucumbers—into evenly sized slices. Try to avoid stacking cheese on top of or below tomato or cucumber. That contributes to the sliding phenomenon because the moist veg will easily slide on the smooth cheese. And lettuce can be a bit tricky too. I recommend cutting out the core from most lettuces before layering them on your sandwich to remove bulk that can cause unevenness.

It's not rocket science, really. And of course, when you're dealing with insane sandwiches, there are always exceptions to the rules. Just remember that keeping your sandwich even will prevent ingredient slippage so you can enjoy it without fear of fillings landing on your shirt.

event
wiches

9

Home for the holidays? Guests over for game night? Or just thinking about what to get your honey? Don't be a bore with party mixes or last-minute gifts. For a change, put together some Eventwiches for your next celebration. Because no matter what the occasion, it's always a great time for insanewiches.

The Dadwich

Rather than getting Dad yet another tie this Father's Day, fix him this tie-shaped torpedo instead. It's much tastier than its fabric counterpart and is sure to elicit office-wide envy from the dads who got coffee mugs (again) this year. Grilled steak, Swiss, cheddar, and fried onions—what dad wouldn't love that?

NOTE: The tie sandwich used in this picture was freakin' huge! The template included here reflects a scaled-down version.

You'll Need:

- **2** large pieces soft flatbread or pita
- **2** tablespoons olive oil
- **1** small yellow onion, sliced
  salt and pepper to taste
- **¼** teaspoon paprika
- **1** 5-ounce strip loin steak
- **2** slices yellow cheddar
- **2** slices Gouda

Instruments:

Cast-iron grill pan, nonstick skillet, oven mitts, tongs, chopping board, chef's knife, kitchen shears

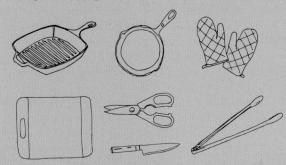

Assembly:

1. Place grill pan in oven under broiler for at least 10 minutes, until hot.

2. Meanwhile, using the template provided in this recipe and the bread-carving technique described on page 17, cut out the bread shape required for this sandwich (tie).

3. Add 1 tablespoon olive oil to nonstick skillet over medium heat.

4. Add onions, salt, pepper, and paprika and sauté for 5–7 minutes or until soft. Set aside.

5. Lightly coat steak with olive oil and season with salt and pepper.

6. Using oven mitts, carefully remove grill pan from oven and place steak in pan. Place back in oven under the broiler for 3–4 minutes, remove, flip steak with tongs and place back in oven for 3 more minutes.

7. Remove grill pan from oven and let steak rest on a separate plate.

8. After the steak has rested for a few minutes, place it on chopping board and slice thin with chef's knife.

9. Place first piece of bread on a plate and assemble as follows: slices of yellow cheddar, steak, Gouda, onions.

10. Top sandwich with second piece.

11. Some cheese will most likely overhang. Using the technique described on page 19 for Cutting Deli Meat Using Shears, cut away any excess cheese.

TEMPLATE

Dad wouldn't have worn the real thing anyway!

Fruitcake Forest

This recipe makes 3 sandwiches

Before you re-gift that fruitcake you received for the holidays, consider using it to make these fruitcake tree sandwiches—orange marmalade with Nutella® makes a deliciously festive combo. They'll be eaten by New Year's, I guarantee it.

You'll Need:

3 teaspoons orange marmalade

6 slices fruitcake, sliced from a loaf

3 teaspoons Nutella

Instruments:

Butter knife, Christmas tree-shaped cookie cutter (3 inches long from top to bottom)

Assembly:

1. Spread 1 teaspoon of marmalade on each of three slices of fruitcake.

2. Spread 1 teaspoon Nutella on each of the remaining slices of fruitcake.

3. Stack a marmalade slice on top of a Nutella slice. Repeat until you have three fruitcake sandwiches.

4. Using the cookie cutter, stamp out one tree from each of the fruitcake sandwiches.

5. Stand each on its tree trunk.

 *Spruce up your holiday feast.*

➤ *Frosty the sandwich was a yummy, happy soul.*

Frosty The Sandwich

Inclement weather should never hold you back from insanewiching. And one of the best cold-weather 'wiches is Frosty here. Just imagine making this one after sledding with the kids and then enjoying it with hot chocolate by the fire. If that isn't a Hallmark holiday moment, I don't know what is.

You'll Need:

6 slices white bread

3 tablespoons apple butter

3 teaspoons strawberry jam

red decorating gel

black decorating gel

1 candy cane

Instruments:

2 spoons, 3½-, 3-, and 2½-inch diameter round cookie cutters

Assembly:

1. Lay down three slices of bread.

2. Spread each slice with 1 tablespoon of apple butter and 1 teaspoon strawberry jam.

3. Top each sandwich with the remaining three slices of bread.

4. Using one of each size cookie cutter per sandwich, stamp out three rounds.

5. Place the large round on the plate as the snowman's bottom, the medium round above it as snowman's torso, and the small round as the snowman's head.

6. Using the red decorating gel, draw eyes, nose, and mouth on the snowman's head.

7. Using the black decorating gel, draw three buttons on snowman's torso.

8. Lay the candy cane beside the snowman, with the curvy part upwards.

The Ghoulish Hand Sandwich

A bit freaked out? You shoulda seen the goblin attached to this hand! That devil would've made your hair stand on end! This savory, severed snack is good fuel for when you wanna stay on guard against all those things that go bump in the night.

You'll Need:

2 white tortilla wraps

1 6-ounce hamsteak (½ inch thick)

10–15 drops red food coloring

3 tablespoons corn syrup

1 chive strand

1 slice Colby cheese

1 tablespoon flour

1 tablespoon water

5 pumpkin seeds

Instruments:

Cutting board, hand-shaped cookie cutter (4 inches long from tip of middle finger to wrist, approximately 4 inches wide), small bowl, kitchen shears, black edible marker

Assembly:

1. Stack two tortilla wraps on a cutting board. Place cookie cutter on top and stamp out two hand-shaped slices.

2. Using the same cookie cutter, stamp a hand shape from the hamsteak.

3. Place one hand-shaped tortilla slice on a plate, place hamsteak hand on top, then top sandwich with second hand-shaped wrap. Make sure the fingers are lined up evenly.

4. In a bowl, mix together food coloring and corn syrup.

5. Holding the sandwich together carefully, dip the wrist into the colored corn syrup to create a severed effect.

6. Place hand back onto plate, making sure a little blood trails.

7. Wrap chive around the middle finger and cut off any excess with kitchen shears.

8. Using the kitchen shears, cut a tiny ¼-inch diameter circle from the Colby cheese and place it on top of the chive to create a ring.

9. Mix the flour with water and dab a little on the tips of each finger.

10. Place a pumpkin seed on the tip of each finger. The flour-water mix will act as an adhesive and hold the pumpkin seed fingernails in place.

11. Draw knuckles using the black edible marker.

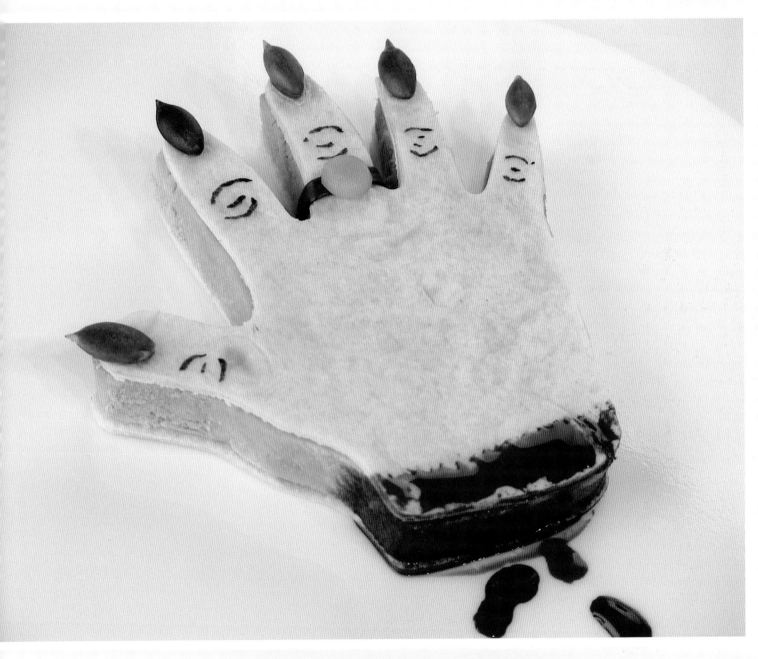

Need a Halloween lunch idea? Let me give you a hand.

The Pumpkin Cheeseburger

Under normal circumstances, it's rude to stick your tongue out. But who could scold this cute sandwich for being saucy? When everyone else is carving creepy, scary jack-o'-lanterns, put this sassy squash on your front step.

NOTE: *This is a craft sandwich and is not to be eaten. Use it to entertain the kids and neighbors on Halloween!*

You'll Need:

1 slice white cheddar

1 small gourd or squash

1 tablespoon canola oil

1 burger patty (homemade or store bought)

2 Boston lettuce leaves

2 slices tomato

2 dabs mustard

Instruments:

Apple corer, chef's knife, cast iron skillet, spatula, two googly eyes, red edible marker

Assembly:

1. Using the template provided with this recipe and the bread-carving technique described on page 17, cut out the shape required for the tongue from the cheese.

2. Using the apple corer, stamp out two circles from the remaining cheese.

3. Carefully slice gourd in half lengthwise using chef's knife. Scoop out and reserve seeds.

4. Add 1 tablespoon canola oil to a cast iron skillet over medium heat. Place burger patty in hot oil and cook on both sides for 5–7 minutes. Set aside.

5. Place lettuce leaves on the bottom half of the gourd.

6. Layer tomato slices and burger patty on top of the lettuce.

7. Top sandwich with the other half of the gourd. Place some reserved seeds on top.

8. Dab mustard on each cheddar cheese circle and affix them to the top gourd half as eyes. Place the googly eyes on top of the cheddar circles. The moisture from the cheese will keep them in place.

9. Using the red edible marker, draw one line down the center of the tongue.

10. Insert base end of tongue in between the burger patty and top half of the gourd.

TEMPLATE

Oh, Gourd, yer so silly!

Prepare to eat a sandwich unlike any you've feared before!

Step 3

Step 4

Step 5

Step 6

Step 7

The Blair Sandwich Project

Maybe you should think twice about picnicking in the woods with this sandwich. You could end up like those three youngsters from that movie who disappeared while hiking. If you're not careful, a simple lunchtime snack could become an excursion into tasty 'wich terror!

You'll Need:

3 slim 12-inch pepperoni sticks

1 small tortilla wrap

1 tablespoon mustard

Instruments:

Chef's knife, 4 toothpicks, kitchen shears, chopping board

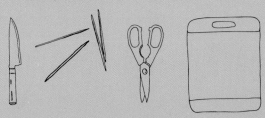

Assembly:

1. Cut the pepperoni sticks to 7 inches in length.

2. Using the excess from one pepperoni stick, cut one more 4-inch length stick.

3. Take two of the larger pepperoni sticks and criss-cross them so there is more length at the bottom. Where the sticks meet, insert a toothpick.

4. Cut the tips of the sticks off on an angle so the horizontal stick will rest flat.

5. Lay the horizontal stick on top and insert two toothpicks diagonally so the stick is attached.

6. Lay the 4-inch piece behind the top of the structure and insert a toothpick where it meets the horizontal stick.

7. Cut the excess toothpicks off with kitchen shears.

8. From the tortilla wrap, cut several ¼-inch strips.

9. Lay the strips along the pepperoni sticks. Some strips will need to be cut into smaller bits to fit along the pepperoni sticks.

10. Dab a little bit of mustard behind each strip so they will adhere to the structure.

11. Adhere strips to the pepperoni stick structure.

NOTE: Please remove toothpicks before eating.

Along Came A Sandwich

Eeeeek! Somebody call the exterminator! Oh, wait. Those are just Halloween spiderwiches made to look like creepy crawlies. Yum! Now those critters don't look icky at all.

You'll Need:

- **4** thin chocolate wafer cookies
- **1** small tube of white frosting
- **32** inches of red string licorice (cut into 8 equal pieces)
- **32** inches of grape string licorice (cut into 8 equal pieces)
- **2** yellow Smarties®
- **2** red Smarties

Instruments:

Kitchen shears

Assembly:

1. Lay down two of the chocolate cookies on your counter.
2. Using the tube of frosting, pipe a layer onto each cookie, covering the entire cookie.
3. Top each cookie with one of the remaining two cookies.
4. For the first cookie sandwich: Poke four pieces of red string licorice into one side and four into the other.
5. For the second cookie sandwich: Poke four pieces of grape string licorice into one side and four into the other.
6. Place the two yellow Smartie eyes on the upper portion of the red-legged spider and the red Smartie eyes on the upper portion of the grape-legged spider.

➤ *To cure sandwich arachnophobia, eat these guys for lunch.*

G'head, hun, unwrap it!

The Giftwich

Can't decide what to get for your honey's birthday? Try this Reuben with a ribbon. It makes the perfect gift when you're trying to impress your significant other. 'Cuz what else says "I love you" like pastrami and Swiss on rye?

You'll Need:

3 slices rye bread (the largest you can find)

28 slices pastrami (the largest you can find)

4 slices Swiss cheese

Instruments:

Bread knife, chef's knife, length of ribbon (approx. 20 inches long), kitchen shears, ribbon bow

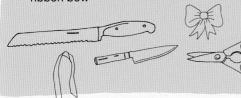

Assembly:

1. Stack rye slices and cut all at once to form three squares approximately 4 by 4 inches.

2. Stack the pastrami into four piles of seven slices and cut each stack into a square 4 inches by 4 inches.

3. Stack four slices of Swiss cheese and cut the stack into a square 4 inches by 4 inches.

4. On a plate, stack as follows: slice of bread, first stack of meat, slice of cheese, second stack of meat, second slice of cheese, second slice of bread, third stack of meat, third slice of cheese, fourth stack of meat, fourth slice of cheese, last slice of bread.

5. Wrap the ribbon around the sandwich and cut off the excess with shears.

6. Hide the knot on top with the bow.

The Easter Feaster

Bunnies are too cute to eat. So last Easter, I skipped the cottontail-shaped sammy and made this colored egg 'wich. Since I've never seen an egg frolic in a field or go hippity-hop, I had no problems at all devouring this one.

You'll Need:

2 slices white bread

¼ green bell pepper

¼ yellow bell pepper

¼ red bell pepper

2 leaves loose leaf lettuce

2 eggs, hardboiled, peeled, sliced

3 ounces cooked, shredded leg of lamb

Instruments:

Chef's knife

Assembly:

1. Using the template provided and the bread-carving technique described on page 17, cut out the shape required for this sandwich (Easter egg) from the bread.

2. Prep bell peppers in advance: skin the green, yellow and red bell peppers using the technique described on page 19.

3. Using the chef's knife, cut a ¼-inch thick strip from the green bell pepper that's about 2½ inches long.

4. Using the chef's knife, cut a ¼-inch thick strip from the yellow bell pepper that's about 3½ inches long.

5. Using the chef's knife, cut a ¼-inch thick strip from the red bell pepper that's about 3½ inches long. Cut into five small squares.

6. Optional: If you'd like to give the egg a more rounded appearance, you can cut each bell pepper strip into an arch, making each slightly rounded instead of perfectly straight.

7. Lay one slice of bread on the plate, layer on lettuce, eggs, lamb; top with second slice of bread.

8. Lay the green pepper strip horizontally on the top slice of bread approximately 1 inch from the top edge of the slice. Lay the yellow pepper strip horizontally 1 inch below the green pepper strip, and lay the red squares horizontally 1 inch below the yellow pepper strip

TEMPLATE

Anyone up for an Easter egg
'wich hunt?

Cook to the beat of a different drumstick.

⬎ TEMPLATES ⬍

The Happy Thankwich

Still feelin' peeved 'cuz cousin Sally stole the last drumstick? You can get over this horrible Thanksgiving Day tragedy by making a drumstick-shaped sandwich from the leftovers you took home. If Sally finds out you made it, she'll be envious!

You'll Need:

1 tablespoon olive oil

½ small onion, chopped

2 slices bacon, fried crisp, chopped

1 tablespoon fresh thyme, chopped

salt and pepper to taste

2 slices light rye bread, cubed

2 slices dark rye bread

2 slices white bread

3–4 ounces cooked turkey breast, chopped

4–5 tablespoons cranberry sauce (store bought or homemade)

cooked peas and corn

Instruments:

Cast-iron pan, chef's knife, spoon

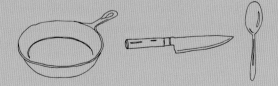

Assembly:

NOTE: *If there's leftover stuffing from your Thanksgiving meal, feel free to use it for this sandwich, but in case it was all devoured, I've included steps for making it homemade.*

1. Heat olive oil in a cast-iron pan over medium heat, add onions and sauté for 2 minutes.

2. Add bacon, thyme, salt, pepper, and cubed pieces of light rye bread, and sauté mixture for about 7 minutes or until golden. Set stuffing mix aside.

3. Using the templates provided and the bread-carving technique described on page 17, cut out the shapes required for this sandwich (drumstick meat and bone. The meat portion of the drumstick is formed with the dark rye and the bone portion is formed with the white bread).

4. Take one meat shape and one bone shape and lay them next to each other on a plate so that the narrowest part of the meat shape butts up against the narrow end of the bone shape.

5. On top of the meat and bone shapes, layer on the leftover turkey breast (if you like yours warm, feel free to microwave it).

6. On top of the turkey breast, spread the stuffing mix, which should still be warm.

7. Finally, spoon cranberry sauce over the stuffing.

8. Top the sandwich with the second drumstick meat and bone shapes.

9. Serve with additional cranberry sauce, stuffing, peas, and corn.

Corned Beef and Cabbage on Clover Leaf Bread

Quite frankly, I find leprechauns a bit creepy. Don't you? To avoid a serious case of the heebie-jeebies on St. Patty's Day, try this clover design instead. It's guaranteed not to cause the willies!

You'll Need:

2 slices caraway seed whole wheat bread

4 ounces savoy cabbage

salt

3 ounces deli-style corned beef

Instruments:

Pot, strainer, chopping board, chef's knife

Assembly:

1. Using the template provided and the bread-carving technique described on page 17, cut out the shape required for this sandwich (clover) from the bread.

2. Place cabbage in pot of boiling salted water for 8 minutes, drain with strainer, and chop roughly.

3. Microwave corned beef for 2 minutes, then chop roughly.

4. Place the first slice of bread on a plate and layer the corned beef and the cabbage on top of it.

5. Top the sandwich with the second slice of bread.

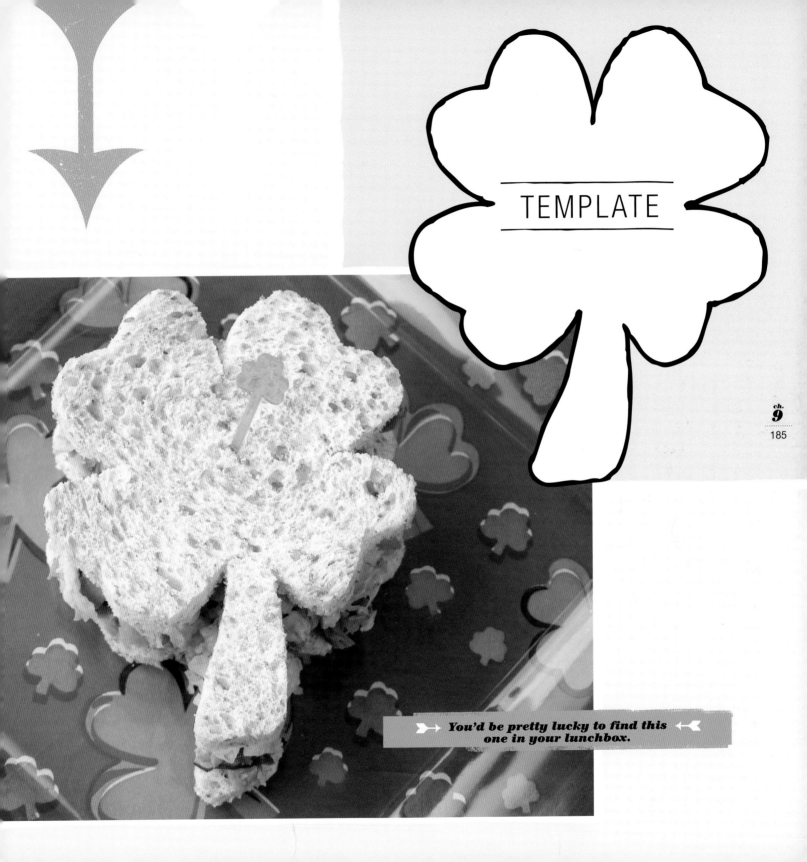

TEMPLATE

➤➤ *You'd be pretty lucky to find this* ◄◄
one in your lunchbox.

And The Winner Is…'Wich

Roaring thunder and all-day neck turning can sure build up an appetite. But if you plan ahead, you'll have some very interesting insanewiches packed away. Each racetrack-inspired hoagie contains manual cheese transmission, pretzel axles, and kielbasa rear-wheel drive. They'll help you steer clear of hunger.

You'll Need:

- **2** 8-inch hoagie buns
- **4** slices Colby cheese
- **4** large slices corned beef
- **1** slice mortadella, without fat chunks (ask for it to be cut ½ inch thick at the deli counter)
- **4** slices kielbasa (about ½ inch thick each)
- **4** slices Italian salami (2 inches in diameter, each cut about ½ inch thick)
- **8** pretzel sticks
- **2** slices chorizo

    mustard (for adhesive)

Instruments:

Bread knife, steak knife, tablespoon, kitchen shears, chopping board, wooden skewer, 3 colored toothpicks

Assembly (makes two):

1. With your bread knife, slice one bun lengthwise.

2. Lay two slices each of Colby cheese and corned beef on the bottom slice, then using the technique on page 19, cut away overhanging meat and cheese with your kitchen shears. Reserve excess corned beef.

3. Next, carve a U-shaped segment (cockpit) out of the top slice of the bun using the steak knife. Make sure it's closer to the back end.

4. With your spoon, scoop out any excess bread in the cockpit and then use this slice to top the sandwich.

5. Using the templates provided in this recipe and the carving technique described on page 17, cut out the shapes required for this sandwich from the mortadella slice. (Driver's backrest and seat respectively). **NOTE:** *One slice of mortadella is large enough to make the backrest and seat for two cars.*

6. Place the mortadella backrest and seat into the cockpit.

7. Poke a hole in the center of each kielbasa slice using the skewer. Do the same with the front-wheel salami wheels.

8. Poke a pretzel stick into each of the wheels so that ½ inch of pretzel is showing on one side and 2 inches of pretzel is sticking out on the other side.

9. Slide the kielbasa wheels into the back end of the hotrod between the two bread slices and the salami wheels into the front end

continued ➤

between the two bread slices.

10. Next, cut out your favorite number with the excess corned beef and stick it onto the side of the bun using small dabs of mustard as adhesive.

11. Poke half a toothpick through the center of your chorizo slice. Stick it into the dashboard to create the hoagie's steering wheel and column. One chorizo link is enough to make a steering wheel for two cars.

12. Finally, poke a full toothpick into the sandwich's back end to create an antenna.

13. Repeat steps 1 through 12 to construct the second car-shaped insanewich.

TEMPLATES

Backrest

Seat

Gentlemen, start your...sandwiches?

Step 3

Step 8

The Gridiron Grinder

Pizza. Wings. Chili. Been there, ate that. This Superbowl, dare to be different by tossing this football hero onto your guests' plates. While the NFL'ers are huddling around the pigskin, you'll be serving pork loin, apples, onions, and bleu cheese on football rye. Guaranteed high fives all around.

You'll Need:

- **2** slices dark rye bread
- **2** tablespoons butter
- **½** large white onion, sliced
  salt and pepper to taste
- **1** small Royal Gala apple, peeled, cored and diced
- **¼** teaspoon powdered nutmeg
- **¼** teaspoon powdered cinnamon
- **1** tablespoon honey
- **1** 4-ounce boneless loin pork chop, approximately ½ inch thick.
- **1** tablespoon olive oil
- **2** ounces bleu cheese, crumbled

Instruments:

Nonstick skillet, cast-iron skillet, baking sheet, chef's knife

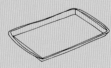

Assembly:

1. Using the template provided in this recipe and the bread-carving technique described on page 17, cut out the shape required for this sandwich (football) from the bread.

2. Melt 1 tablespoon of butter in a nonstick skillet over medium-low heat. Add onions, reserving two raw slices, and sauté until caramelized, about 8 minutes. Add salt and pepper to taste. Remove cooked onion from skillet and set aside.

3. In the same skillet, melt remaining butter over medium-low heat and add apple. Sauté for 5 minutes, then add nutmeg, cinnamon, and honey. Sauté for an additional 3 minutes and set aside.

4. Preheat cast-iron skillet on stovetop over medium heat for 8 minutes. Meanwhile, preheat oven to 400°F.

5. Season pork chop with salt and pepper. Add olive oil to hot cast-iron skillet and place pork chop in pan. Cook on each side for 3 minutes. Remove from skillet and set aside.

6. Place one slice of dark rye bread on a baking sheet and stack with the cooked onions, pork chop, apple, and bleu cheese. Place in oven for 4 minutes or until bleu cheese has melted.

7. Remove from oven and transfer to plate. Top with second slice of rye bread.

8. Cut one sliver of reserved raw onion into three equal lengths and place on top of sandwich horizontally to mimic cross stitching. Place the other reserved onion sliver vertically over the three lengths to complete the stitching effect.

Kick off the big game feast with this.

TEMPLATE

Insanewich Field

Before the coin toss and kickoff, prepare this field goal flank steak quesadilla to get everyone in sporting spirit. When flank steak is cooked medium rare and sliced thin, it's enough to make any hungry fan drool. And the anticipation is only intensified when the sandwich resembles a football field!

You'll Need:

FIELD GOAL POSTS:

4 slim 12-inch pepperoni sticks

2 slices Italian salami (2 inches in diameter, each cut about ¾ inch thick)

FOOTBALL FIELD:

2 tablespoons butter

½ medium sweet onion, diced

2 ounces red bell pepper, diced

2 ounces yellow bell pepper, diced

2 ounces orange bell pepper, diced

6 ounces flank steak

1 tablespoon olive oil

salt and pepper to taste

2 spinach tortilla wraps

4 slices Monterey Jack cheese

1 white tortilla wrap

1 tomato tortilla wrap

Instruments:

Chef's knife, chopping board, 8 toothpicks, kitchen shears, nonstick skillet, cast-iron skillet, baking sheet, spatula

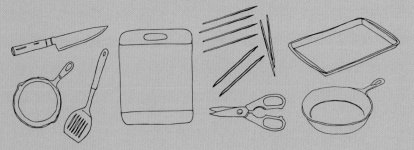

Field Goal Post Assembly:

1. Cut two lengths from one pepperoni stick each approximately 4 inches long for the bottom portion of the field goal posts.

2. Cut two lengths from one pepperoni stick each approximately 3 inches long for the crossbar portions of the field goal posts.

3. Cut four more lengths from the two remaining pepperoni sticks, each approximately 3 inches long, to form two sets of upright posts.

4. Insert toothpicks for each field goal post as shown using one slice of salami for each as the base.

5. Cut off the excess toothpicks with kitchen shears.

6. Place both posts in fridge while constructing the field.

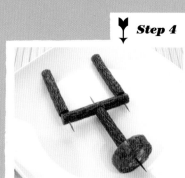

▼ Step 4

> **The tastiest part is the line of scrimmich!**

Football Field Assembly:

1. Melt butter in a nonstick skillet over medium heat. Add onion and sauté for 2 minutes. Add red, yellow, and orange bell pepper and sauté for an additional 5 minutes. Set aside.

2. Preheat oven to 400°F. On stove top, preheat cast-iron skillet over high heat for 8 minutes.

3. Lightly coat flank steak with olive oil, season both sides with salt and pepper. Place flank steak in hot cast-iron skillet and sear both sides for 2 minutes to achieve a brown crust. Finish cooking steak in oven for approximately 4 minutes to achieve medium rare. Remove from oven and let rest on a separate plate for at least 5 minutes.

4. Meanwhile, cut two stacked spinach tortillas into rectangles approximately 6 inches by 8 inches.

5. Place one tortilla on a baking sheet and spread onion and bell pepper mixture over top.

6. Slice the flank steak thin going against the grain and layer on top of onion and pepper mixture.

7. Layer slices of cheese over the steak and top with the second spinach tortilla to form the quesadilla.

8. Cut two strips from the white tortilla approximately ¾ inch thick and 6 inches long. Place on top of the quesadilla at either end to denote end zones.

9. Cut one strip from the tomato tortilla approximately ¾ inch thick and 6 inches long. Place on top of the quesadilla along the center to denote the 50-yard line.

10. Place baking sheet back in preheated oven for 4 minutes or until cheese is melted.

11. Carefully remove insanewich with long spatula and place on a large serving tray.

12. Remove field goal posts from fridge and place at either end of the field.

Makin' Sweet Potato Lovewich

This ain't called the "lovewich" for nothin': prepare this one and it will have your sweetheart mooning over you like the day you first locked eyes on each other. Be forewarned that eating this may cause unadulterated feelings of intense joy and butterflies in your stomach.

You'll Need:

	salt to taste
6	fresh green beans
1	teaspoon olive oil
1	large white potato
1	large sweet potato
1	tablespoon butter
	splash of milk
½	tablespoon chopped chive
	pepper to taste
	pinch of cinnamon
	pinch of nutmeg
1	tablespoon honey

Instruments:

2 pots, potato masher, 2 bowls, heart-shaped cookie cutter (3 inches top to bottom and 3½ inches left to right at the widest point), spatula

Assembly:

1. In a pot of boiling salted water, boil green beans for 3 minutes, and drain water, leaving beans in pot. Add olive oil to coat. Cover and set aside, away from heat.

2. Boil one large white potato, drain, peel, and mash. Set aside in bowl.

3. Boil one large sweet potato, drain, peel, and mash. Set aside in separate bowl.

4. Add ½ tablespoon butter, milk, chives, salt, and pepper to the white potato mash.

5. Add ½ tablespoon butter, cinnamon, nutmeg, salt, and honey to sweet potato mash.

6. Place heart-shaped cookie cutter on a plate and fill it with the white potato mash.

7. Lift the cookie cutter to release the mash in a heart shape.

8. Once again, place cleaned heart-shaped cookie cutter on a plate and fill it with the sweet potato mash. Lift the cookie cutter to release the mash in a heart shape.

9. Using a spatula, gently lift the white potato heart and place it in the center of a plate.

10. Layer beans over top.

11. Using a spatula, gently lift the sweet potato heart and place it on top of the green beans.

When you make this sandwich for Valentine's Day, put your heart into it.

Up Shiitake Creek

This Valentine's Day sandwich could help you make up for botched birthdays or forgotten anniversaries. It's got shiitake mushrooms and scrambled eggs on French bread—tasty ingredients that could help you smooth things over. Serve it on Februrary 14th and you could avoid being up the creek without a paddle!

You'll Need:

- **1** yellow bell pepper, diced
- **2** tablespoons olive oil
- **2** dashes red wine vinegar

  salt to taste
- **1** red bell pepper, diced
- **1** ounce shiitake mushrooms, chopped (reserve one whole)

  pepper to taste
- **1** egg
- **2** tablespoons milk
- **3** slices brioche bread or challah

Instruments:

3 bowls, chef's knife, small heart-shaped cookie cutter, nonstick skillet, fork, 2½-inch diameter round cookie cutter

Assembly:

1. In a bowl combine yellow bell pepper, ½ tablespoon olive oil, dash of red wine vinegar, and salt.

2. In another bowl combine red bell pepper, ½ tablespoon olive oil, dash of red wine vinegar, and salt.

3. Make sure to reserve one quarter of the red bell pepper and skin it following the directions on page 19.

4. Using the heart cookie cutter, stamp a small heart shape from the skinned red bell pepper.

5. Heat ½ tablespoon of olive oil in a nonstick skillet over medium heat.

6. Add chopped mushrooms and reserved whole mushroom, salt and pepper and sauté for 4–5 minutes. Remove from skillet and set aside.

7. In a small bowl, beat egg and milk with fork until fully incorporated.

8. Heat ½ tablespoon of olive oil in a nonstick skillet over medium-low heat. Add egg mixture and scramble. Remove from heat and set aside.

9. Using the round cookie cutter, stamp one round from each slice of bread.

10. Stack the sandwich as follows: one slice of bread, the egg, the second bread slice, the chopped mushroom, the third bread slice.

11. Place the red bell pepper heart and reserved whole shiitake mushroom on top.

12. Serve on top of or beside the bell pepper salads.

The meal you make if you messed up!

Meet the sweet dream team of sammies.

Sleepover Sandwiches

If you need to feed some diehard slumber partiers, these playful peanut butter and apple 'wiches will fit the bill. The apples are a fun and healthy alternative to the usual bread slices. My nieces (ages eight and eleven) enjoy these while playing games or listening to music at a sleepover.

You'll Need:

- **1** red apple
- **1** green apple
- **2** tablespoons creamy peanut butter

Instruments:

Chef's knife, chopping board, small heart-shaped cookie cutter, butter knife

Assembly:

1. Cut two ½-inch slices from red apple and two ½-inch slices from green apple.

2. Remove core from each slice using cookie cutter, leaving a heart-shaped hole.

3. Spread 1 tablespoon of peanut butter onto one red apple slice and 1 tablespoon of peanut butter onto one green slice. *NOTE: when you spread the peanut butter, excess will likely fall through the heart-shaped hole. This is OK.*

4. Top each peanut butter slice with its respective color slice.

dessert
wiches

10

Staying on track with your healthy eating plan sure is a drag sometimes, don't ya think? Sweet treats seem to call your name at your weakest moments. We've all been there. But it doesn't mean you can't indulge once in a while. Sometimes you just gotta treat yourself to a sweet Dessertwich.

Banana Splitwich

Ever wonder what a banana split would look like in sandwich form? Here it is. With rounds of banana bread teetering on layers of banana and ice cream, it's sure not the same split you had as a kid.

You'll Need:

3 slices store-bought banana bread

2 scoops vanilla ice cream

½ banana

dollop whipped cream

3 tablespoons chocolate sauce

Instruments:

3-inch diameter round cookie cutter, ice cream scoop, spoon, chef's knife

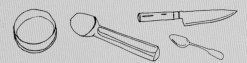

Assembly:

1. Using the round cookie cutter, stamp out one round from each slice of banana bread. Place in freezer.

2. Place the round cookie cutter on a large plate and place one scoop of vanilla ice cream onto it.

3. Pat the ice cream down with a spoon to create a disk shape. Gently lift the cutter to release it from the ice cream.

4. Repeat steps 2 and 3 on the same plate to form a second ice cream disk. Place plate in freezer for at least 1 hour or until ice cream is very firm to the touch.

5. Before you are ready to assemble the splitwich, cut banana half lengthwise in quarters.

6. Remove bread and ice cream from freezer and stack on a plate as follows: bread round, ice cream disk, banana quarter, bread round, ice cream disk, banana quarter, bread round, dollop of whipped cream.

7. Pour chocolate sauce on top.

**When you want a decadent dessert,
you gotta go full tilt!**

The Rice Cream Sandwich

Normally, rice cakes are kinda healthy. But come on, you can easily transform those babies into a sinful 'wich by adding vanilla ice cream. Sure, it's devious, but you know you want it!

You'll Need:

2 rice cakes

2 scoops vanilla ice cream

Instruments:

Ice cream scoop, toothpick

Assembly:

1. Place first rice cake on plate.

2. Scoop ice cream on top of first rice cake.

3. Top sandwich with second rice cake.

4. Poke toothpick into the middle of top rice cake.

➤ *Rice cakes, meet your arch NOMesis!*

> ➤ *How does it taste? It's money.*

Penny For Your Thoughtwich

If this penny-sized 'wich could talk, it'd say: "Hey Abe, turn around and check out how yummy I am. You'll love my yogurt and honey filling and my sweet eyes. Abe, you listening?"

You'll Need:

2 Chex® cereal pieces

1 teaspoon yogurt

1 teaspoon honey

2 white mini confectioner's disks (can be found in the baking aisle at the grocery store)

1 pink mini confectioner's disk

red frosting

Assembly:

1. Place one Chex piece on plate.

2. In a cup, mix the yogurt and honey and spoon mixture onto the first Chex piece.

3. Top sandwich with second Chex piece.

4. Place white mini confectioner's disks on the top Chex as eyeballs.

5. Dab red frosting onto each eyeball to create the pupils.

6. Cut one pink mini confectioner's disk in half with the steak knife and place on the top Chex piece to form the upper and lower lip.

Instruments:

Cup, spoon, steak knife

Where no sandwich has gone before...

Beam-Me-Up-Scotty Sandwich

There's a mixed drink called "The Beam Me Up Scotty," which contains coffee liquor, crème de bananes, and Irish cream. This sandwich version's got slices of banana on Irish cream-soaked coffee cake and Mr. Spock on the side.

You'll Need:

2 slices store-bought marble coffee cake

1 small banana, sliced

½ shot of Irish cream liqueur

Instruments:

Bread knife, chef's knife

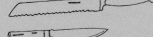

Assembly:

1. Place first slice of coffee cake on plate.
2. Layer slices of banana on top of first slice.
3. Top sandwich with second slice of coffee cake
4. Pour liqueur over sandwich.
5. Eat immediately.

The Boston Massacre Burger

It's a massacre because, well, just look at the sweet carnage: Two mint patty burgers, smooshed Starburst® cheese, Boston cream mayo, and colored coconut lettuce all on a Boston cream donut bun. Oh, the horror! The dizzyingly sweet horror!

You'll Need:

- **2** store-bought Boston cream donuts
- **10** orange Starburst candies
- **2** ounces shredded coconut
- **15** drops green food coloring
- **2** peppermint patties
- **1** teaspoon sesame seeds

Instruments:

Chef's knife, spoon, microwave-safe plate, chopping board, 3-inch square cookie cutter, 2 bowls

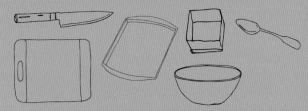

Assembly:

1. Slice two Boston cream donuts in half with chef's knife and scoop out the custard into a bowl using the spoon. Set aside one donut.

2. Unwrap ten Starburst candies and place in microwave on oven proof plate for 25–30 seconds to make them pliable.

3. While they are still warm, roll melted candy into a ball with clean hands, then smoosh the whole mass into a flat sheet on the chopping board.

4. Using the cookie cutter, stamp a square out of the Starburst sheet and remove the excess.

5. Place coconut in a small bowl and mix in food coloring.

6. Assemble burger as follows: bottom half of one donut, first mint patty, Starburst cheese, half of the custard, second mint patty, second half of the custard, shredded coconut, top half of donut sprinkled with sesame seeds.

A deliciously grisly scene.

Great for Kids!

Muffin-Top Monster

Yikes! Is that a big pimply nose and festering teeth!? Or a red jujube and green jelly beans? Either way, they're attached to a pretty creepy-looking beast! Watch out kids, 'cuz this muffin monster could be hiding under your bed!

You'll Need:

2 large store-bought muffins, any flavor

2 tablespoons almond butter

6 green jelly beans

1 red jujube

small tube of green frosting

2 green Froot Loops®

8 strands fiber cereal (Kellogg's® All-Bran®)

Instruments:

Bread knife, spoon, toothpick

Assembly:

1. Cut the tops off two muffins using the bread knife.

2. Flip one muffin top over so the rounded side is facing down.

3. Spread with almond butter using spoon.

4. Line jelly beans along the front edge of the flipped muffin top.

5. Place the second muffin top on top of the jelly beans so the rounded part is facing up.

6. Poke a toothpick into the jujube.

7. Stick the jujube into the upper muffin top as the nose.

8. Dab frosting onto each Froot Loop so they will adhere, and place them onto the upper muffin top as eyes.

9. Above each eye, place four fiber cereal strands as the eyebrows.

ch.
10

207

Monster Mods

Here are some other tidbits you can use to modify this monstrous dessert:

Eyebrows: Hickory sticks (for a nice sweet and salty contrast!)

Eyes: Lucky Charms®, Coco Puffs®, Gummies® Life Savers

Nose: Sour peach, sour watermelon, large gumdrop, nibs

Teeth: Smarties, candy corn, mini-marshmallows, chocolate mini-eggs

*Wanna make others yellow with envy:
Eat this in front of them.*

The Lemon Sorbwich

Nothin' but lemony goodness all-round with this one, peeps. Lemon cake and lemon sorbet sammiched between a real lemon: If that doesn't get yer lips all puckered up in a good way, I dunno what will!

You'll Need:

2 slices of store-bought lemon pound cake

1 lemon

2 scoops lemon sorbet

sprig of mint

Instruments:

2½-inch diameter round cookie cutter, chef's knife, glass bowl, ice cream scoop

Assembly:

1. Using the cookie cutter, stamp one round from each slice of cake.

2. Slice the lemon in half and then slice a small ¼-inch slice from the bottom half's tip so it will stand in the bowl. Place the bottom half of the lemon in the glass bowl.

3. Place one scoop of lemon sorbet on top of the bottom lemon half, then one cake round, a second scoop and a second round.

4. Top the sandwich with the top half of lemon and add a sprig of mint.

Dangling Donut 'N' Coffee Sandwich

Just look at the little squirt, hanging out there, showing off its peanut butter and blueberry jam filling. It won't be long before it's inhaled by one of the countless folks who start their day off with a coffee and donut.

You'll Need:

1 cup hot coffee

3 mini powdered donuts

3 teaspoons peanut butter

3 teaspoons blueberry jam

Instruments:

Steak knife, spoon, stir stick

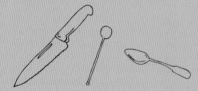

Assembly:

1. Slice each mini-donut in half with the steak knife.

2. On the bottom halves of each, spread one teaspoon of peanut butter and one teaspoon of blueberry jam.

3. Top each little donut sandwich with their respective top halves.

4. Pour the coffee into a cup and dip the stir stick into the liquid.

5. Choose one donut and slide the stir stick through its hole, then rest the donut on the cup's rim.

6. Serve the other two donuts alongside the coffee on a small plate.

➤➤ *These little fellas cause quite a stir!*

Coffee 'N' Cakewich

I've met more than a few high-strung caffeine addicts who would enjoy this 'wich. With potent coffee custard, this creation is a perfect pick-me-up after that big lunch. In fact, it may have you humming right through the afternoon.

You'll Need:

- **2** cups coffee
- **1** tablespoon cornstarch
- **2** tablespoons sugar
- **3** slices store-bought angel food cake
- **5** large strawberries, sliced

  dollop of whipped cream

  sprig of mint

Instruments:

Mug, spoon, saucepan, round cookie cutter (**NOTE:** *size of cookie cutter will depend on the diameter of your coffee cup*), glass coffee cup

Assembly:

1. Pour about half a cup of coffee into a mug and chill in the fridge.

2. Once the mug is chilled, remove from fridge and add cornstarch. Mix thoroughly with spoon to make a coffee slurry.

3. For the coffee custard: Take the unchilled coffee and add it to a saucepan over medium heat. When it comes to a boil, add sugar. Stir until the sugar is dissolved and then slowly stream in the cornstarch slurry. Keep stirring until the mixture thickens, then turn heat to low. Stir occasionally to prevent skin from forming. Remove from heat about 5 minutes before starting step 5.

4. Using the round cookie cutter, stamp out one round from each of the cake slices.

5. Layer into the glass coffee cup as follows: one slice cake, half of the sliced strawberries, a layer of coffee custard, the second slice of cake, the second half of the sliced strawberries, another layer of custard, the last slice of cake, a dollop of whipped cream and a sprig of mint.

Let coffee lovers have their cake
and eat it too!

The Curious Carrot Cake Sandwich

When you look at it, you might think: Whoa! How exactly does one stab a carrot cake sandwich...with a carrot?!? Actually, it's not hard to do. Read on to find out how you can play this dessert-time joke on your friends and family!

You'll Need:

- **4** slices store-bought carrot cake (from a loaf or a round cake)
- **1** medium-sized carrot
- **5** ounces cream cheese
- **2** ounces butter
- **2** tablespoons confectioner's sugar
- **½** teaspoon vanilla extract

Instruments:

2¾-inch square cookie cutter, chef's knife, 2 toothpicks, bowl, spoon, large Ziploc bag, kitchen shears

Assembly:

1. Using the square cookie cutter, stamp out one square shape from each carrot cake slice. Set aside.

2. Cut carrot on the bias in two places as shown in the picture below and insert one toothpick into each cut end.

3. For the frosting: In a bowl, combine cream cheese, butter, confectioner's sugar, and vanilla extract. Ensure the mix is fully incorporated.

4. Spoon mixture into a large Ziploc bag, squeeze contents to one side, twist the bag tight and cut a ½-inch corner using the kitchen shears.

5. Place one carrot cake slice on a plate and pipe one layer of frosting over top.

6. Repeat previous step two more times, stacking the slices, and top sandwich with the last slice.

7. Insert top portion of carrot into the top of the sandwich on an angle and insert bottom portion of carrot into the side of the sandwich on an angle so it looks like the carrot has pierced the sandwich.

Step 2

It's one sweet trick!

The Mostly Melon Pie Chart Sandwich

This one came to me one day while watching a PowerPoint presentation. The presenter changed slides to reveal a very colorful pie chart when it hit me. Why not a pie chart sandwich?

You'll Need:

1 slice store-bought banana bread

2 ounces each of:
Honeydew melon
Pineapple
Cantaloupe
Watermelon

Instruments:

2½-inch diameter round cookie cutter, edible marker, parchment paper, kitchen shears, chef's knife

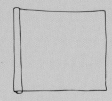

Assembly:

1. Using the cookie cutter, stamp a round from the banana bread slice.

2. Using an edible marker, trace the pie template provided with this recipe on parchment paper.

3. Cut out each pie shape using kitchen shears and use them each as a template to cut out the respective fruit wedges indicated.

4. Make sure each wedge is uniform in thickness. This should give you about a 360-degree total.

5. Place them all on top of the banana bread so the points of each wedge are centered.

Your sweet-toothed friends will fight for a piece of this pie.

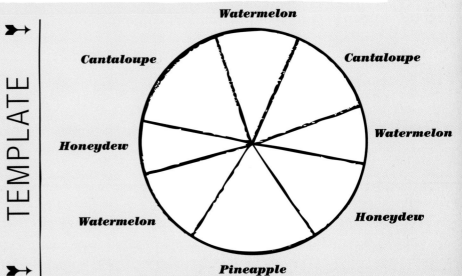

TEMPLATE

Watermelon

Cantaloupe

Cantaloupe

Honeydew

Watermelon

Watermelon

Honeydew

Pineapple

Donut Alarm Clock

You're no doubt wondering how this sandwich is supposed to keep time. But I say the only time you should care about is when you're gonna eat this 'wich. Kiwi cogs, frosting hands, and mini donut alarm bells—how could you wait another minute for that?

You'll Need:

1 chocolate-glazed cake donut or chocolate-frosted donut

3 tablespoons whipped cream

2 kiwis, peeled and sliced

2 mini powdered donuts

1 red jelly bean

2 pieces of black licorice (cut about 3 inches long with shears)

small tubes of pink, green, and blue frosting

Assembly:

1. Slice donut in half horizontally using the bread knife.

2. Using the spoon, dollop whipped cream over the bottom slice and layer the slices of kiwi on top.

3. Top sandwich with the top slice of donut.

4. Using toothpicks affix two mini-donuts to the top of the full-sized donut. Make sure to leave space in between the mini-donuts.

5. Poke a red toothpick into the side of a red jelly bean and pierce the pointed end of the toothpick into the top of the clock in between the mini-donuts.

6. Stick the pieces of black licorice into the bottom of the clock as legs.

7. Draw the hour numbers in pink frosting, the clock hands in green, and put one small dab of blue where the hands meet in the center.

Instruments:

Bread knife, spoon, chef's knife, three toothpicks (one of which must be red), kitchen shears

➤➤ *No snooze button. When it rings,* ◄◄
you gotta eat it.

The Picture-Perfect Cupcake Sandwich

A cupcake sandwich that gets a kid's face all chocolatey with yummy frosting helps make an adorable party snapshot for Mom and Dad. I don't know about you, but I think that's a pretty cute picture!

You'll Need:

- **1** vanilla cupcake, made from store-bought cake mix
- **1** tablespoon store-bought chocolate frosting
- **1** large dollop of marshmallow spread
- **8** pieces of red string licorice (7 about 1 inch in length and 1 about 2 inches)
- **2** purple jelly beans
- **2** yellow mini confectioner's disks (can be found in the baking aisle at the grocery store)
- **1** pink jelly bean
- **2** cashews

Assembly:

1. Make one vanilla cupcake using store-bought cake mix and allow to cool.
2. Spread store-bought chocolate frosting on top of cupcake using the butter knife.
3. Slice the cupcake in half horizontally using the bread knife.
4. Spoon one large dollop of marshmallow spread over the bottom slice and top sandwich with the top slice of the cupcake.
5. Press 7 of the 1-inch string licorice pieces into the top of the head to form the hair.
6. Press two purple jelly beans into the cupcake as eyes and top those eyes with yellow mini confectioner's disks.
7. Cut the pink jelly bean in half using the chef's knife and press the flat side into the cupcake as the nose.
8. Press one cashew into each side of the head to form the ears.
9. Bend the remaining string licorice piece into a "U" shape and press it into the cupcake as the smile.

Instruments:

Butter knife, bread knife, spoon, chef's knife

'Wich Upon A Shooting Star

What crazy skies could have you 'wiching upon puff pastry shooting stars? Only those in your imagination! These cosmic 'wiches are shooting through the night sky with sweet strawberry trailers. With any luck, one will land right on your plate.

You'll Need:

- **1** sheet puff pastry
- cooking spray
- **3** tablespoons honey
- **3** large strawberries

Instruments:

Star-shaped cookie cutter (optional: use different sizes if you like!), baking sheet, steak knife, chef's knife.

NOTE: *Most store-bought puff pastry comes frozen in sheet rolls.*

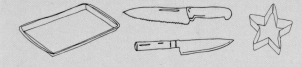

Assembly:

1. Two hours before making this dish, remove puff pastry from freezer and thaw.
2. Preheat oven to 375°F.
3. Unroll puff pastry sheet on a flat surface.
4. Using the cookie cutter, stamp out six star shapes and remove the excess puff pastry.
5. Spray a baking sheet with cooking spray and carefully place stars on sheet.
6. Cook in oven for 12–15 minutes or until stars are puffy and golden.
7. Remove from oven and let cool.
8. When the stars have cooled, slice each one in half using the steak knife.
9. On the bottom half of each star, dab honey to add sweetness and act as an adhesive for the strawberry halves.
10. Cut each large strawberry in half using the chef's knife.
11. Place one half strawberry on each star bottom, making sure that the point end of the strawberry is facing away from the star to mimic the shooting star's trail.
12. Top each little sandwich with its respective star top.

Sandwishes can come true.

Step 8

RESOURCES

Where to Buy:

When gathering materials for insanewiching, you'll be able to find almost all of what you need at a quality cookware store and in the aisles of your local supermarket. But if you need to go online, here are some additional sources:

Cooking.com, **Amazon.com**, and **Williams-Sonoma.com** for basic high-quality, no-brainer implements, utensils and essentials

Cookiecutter.com and **TheCookieCutterShop.com** for all the cookie cutter shapes you'll ever need

Wilton.com for decorating gels and food coloring

Michaels.com for edible markers

FuttersNutButters.com for (you guessed it) nut butters

Deananddeluca.com and **Williams-Sonoma.com** for olive oil, condiments, herbs and spices.

You can also try a few national stores like Crate & Barrel (call 1-800-967-6696 for locations in your area), **Crateandbarrel.com** (in the Kitchen & Food section); Sur La Table (call 1-800-243-0852 for locations in your area), **Surlatable.com**.